Street Machines
Classics ▪ Muscle Cars ▪ Modern

Sue Elliott

First published in 2010 by MBI Publishing Company and Motorbooks, an imprint of MBI Publishing Company, 400 First Avenue North, Suite 300, Minneapolis, MN 55401 USA

Motorbooks titles are also available at discounts in bulk quantity for industrial or sales-promotional use. For details write to Special Sales Manager at MBI Publishing Company, 400 First Avenue North, Suite 300, Minneapolis, MN 55401 USA.

To find out more about our books, visit us online at www.motorbooks.com.

ISBN-13: 978-0-7603-3907-7

Acquiring Editor: Peter Schletty
Project Editor: Carmen Nickisch
Design Manager: Kou Lor
Layout by: Greg Nettles, Squarecrow Creative

Top photo: *Photo courtesy of Classic Recreations*

Second row, left to right: *Photo by DreamCars.com, Photo courtesy of Performance West Group, Photo courtesy of K&N*

Third row, left to right: *Photo courtesy of Chrysler, Photo courtesy of Max Nealon*

Fourth row, left to right: *Photo by Sue Elliott, Photo courtesy of YearOne*

Printed in China

Contents

Introduction

Pro Street. Pro Touring. G-machine. Pro Millenium. Resto-mod. Retro rod.

People keep coming up with terms to try to classify street machines. Yet so many of these highly modified cars and trucks defy classification.

For the purposes of this book, we've loosely defined street machines as 1950-and-newer American cars and trucks . . . with V-8-and-larger engines . . . that have been heavily modified for increased performance and styling. You may spot an earlier vehicle or a twin-turbo V-6 car, but only if it clearly fits into this not-so-clear genre.

Why start with 1950? Well, we had to start somewhere. We had to draw a line in the sand and say, "We'll only include cars built after this year."

In truth, it wasn't easy to pick that starting point, partly because there is no widely accepted definition of *street machine*. But still, we had to focus this title and distinguish it from its sister publication, the *Hot Rods Idea Book*.

Now, one could argue that there are plenty of 1950s vehicles that are really street rods. The distinction I've aimed for here is a focus on serious performance. The cars and trucks in this book were built with an emphasis on acceleration and, in most cases, on handling, as well.

I've been a car magazine editor—and have been writing and doing photography for these titles—for 20-some years now, and it's been fun to watch the enthusiast scene evolve.

When I first starting working on muscle car and Corvette magazines at CSK Publishing Company in New Jersey back in the 1980s, much of the focus

was on 100-point restored cars. People were paying good money to get orange-peel paint jobs, not to mention date-coded spark plug wires and bias-ply tires. At the Bloomington Gold Corvette show, I was amazed to watch people actually spend $3 for a single NOS (new-old-stock) bolt.

Most of the high-dollar cars were trailer queens. Some people even had booties that they would put over the tires and the pedals, so as not to damage their perfect, just-off-the-assembly-line looks while rolling them out of the trailer.

As magazine editors at the time, we begged people to drive their cars and trucks. If they didn't feel comfortable driving their Top Flight Corvettes, then why not build vehicles they could drive?

Now, don't get me wrong. I can appreciate the skill and expertise required to restore a car or truck. I love the fact that people spend the time and money to restore these rolling time capsules—and that more and more people are choosing to maintain perfectly original survivor cars too.

But I guess I'm just a hot rodder at heart. I love street machines because they're meant to be played with. They're built to perform.

Some people want to go really fast in a straight line. Stopping is useful to them. Turning not so important.

Some people want to be able to road race, autocross, and drag race the same car—and take it on a 2,000-mile jaunt across country. I think the fact that people can and do attain this kind of all-around performance—and in a car that looks fantastic too—is both impressive and exciting.

I can still appreciate the desire for throw-you-back-in-your-seat straight-line performance. I, for one, love roasting the tires just for giggles. So, you'll definitely find Pro Street cars and street/strip performers in these pages.

You'll also find cars and trucks that were built to perform in every way, from canyon carving adventurers to skid pad–dominating g-machines.

It's such a joy to point out that while many of the cars and trucks in this book were very expensive to build, they are not trailer queens. They were built to be driven and driven hard.

After thousands of hours of development work, Wraith Motorsports is taking orders for the 1968 Wraith Mustang. The Pro Touring car was designed for street use, drag racing, and road racing. Forget about air conditioning and a stereo. Wraith expects you to listen to the sounds of the 900-horsepower blown 427 FE. *Photo courtesy of Wraith Motorsports*

Garland Miller's 1959 Corvette features a Faerman Racing Engines 385-cubic-inch engine with 10.7:1 compression, Air Flow Research heads, Comp Cams hydraulic roller, Callies crank, Lunati rods, and Autotrend electronic fuel injection. Lakeside Rods and Rides installed the 572-horsepower mill in the car, connecting it to a Keisler PerfectFit TKO 600 manual transmission. *Photo courtesy of Lakeside Rods*

You'll find some very impressive home-built street machines in these pages. But, as it happens, most of these cars and trucks were built by professionals—some big-name builders, some not so well-known—primarily because I focused on vehicles that are truly inspiring. These trend-setting rides will keep the wheels in your head turning for years to come.

As for the *street* in *street machine*, well, all of the vehicles within these pages are streetable, depending on your definition of streetability. After all, everybody's definition is different: Some people require all the creature comforts, from air conditioning to lumbar support; some clearly do not.

I have one friend who would regularly drive his Pro Street '55 Chevy to local cruise nights. The car had a blown, injected big-block Chevy engine that produced 1,025 horsepower on C16 race fuel. It got 1 mile to the gallon (or 1 gallon to the mile, depending on your perspective). With a 15-gallon fuel cell, that gave the car a 15-mile range, give or take. Oh, and it had a spool. Yet he considered it streetable.

The point is this: You may want to suspend your disbelief about a particular car's streetability, because everybody has a different tolerance threshold.

I, for one, really appreciate side mirrors when I'm driving, but a large number of these vehicles have shed them in favor of a smooth, clean look. And I'm quick to admit they do look great.

Bottom line: Even if you wouldn't want to spend 10 minutes in some of the cars and trucks in these pages, I guarantee you'll find ideas worth considering. People have put an incredible amount of thought into envisioning these street machines—and an incredible amount of time into achieving their visions. Some of these cars and trucks have a hundred hours of labor in the bumper modifications alone.

Perhaps most amazing of all is the sheer diversity of vehicles on the scene. Even when you compare two cars built with similar goals and roughly the same starting point—say, two '69 Pro Touring Camaros—you'll find that the end product often turns out radically and delightfully different.

One other phenomenon worth mentioning is the growth in the market for turnkey street machines. While the vast majority of the vehicles in this book are one-offs, you'll find a fair number of cars and trucks that are being produced in limited production runs. Some of them are new cars and trucks, like the Fesler-Moss 2010 Camaro, and some are vintage vehicles, including some '67 Mustangs and '69 Camaros being built with 100 percent new components, thanks to companies like Dynacorn that are offering reproduction bodies.

So, enough back-story. It's time to sit back, flip some pages, and enjoy this tour through the designs and minds of street machine builders. You'll find hundreds of photos that have been selected specifically to inspire you and to help get your creative juices flowing.

The full-length custom console in Modern Muscle's Pro Touring 1969 Camaro is home to battery, temp, fuel, and oil gauges reminiscent of the factory setup, as well as controls for the Electric Life power windows and power door locks. The dash is completely custom. *Photo courtesy of Performance West Group*

1

Chapter 1
Early Street Machines

You'll find that most of the early street machines in this chapter are not 1950 or '51 or '52 models. They were built later. There are more Tri-Five Chevys, early 1960s Ford Starliners, even Chrysler 300s, and Chevy C-10 pickups, not to mention Chevy Biscaynes. That's not because I was discriminating against earlier rides; it's more a factor of what people are building these days.

Also, because the next chapter focuses on muscle cars, this chapter includes all of the cars and trucks that usually are not considered part of that genre (though some Mopar lovers, no doubt, would be happy to debate the point about Chrysler 300s).

I particularly appreciate the preponderance of early Corvette street machines. Not all that long ago, it seemed as if the Corvette scene was all about perfect restorations and NCRS Top Flight judging. People who had the audacity to cut a hole in their fiberglass hoods and stick blowers through them were pretty much pariahs at Corvette shows. But while the restoration hobby is still going strong today, C1 Corvettes have become a hot commodity on the street machine scene. There's even growing interest in the midyear Corvettes.

I have no doubt that the boundaries of what is and is not a street machine will continue to stretch—and this genre that already defies definition will become even more indefinable—as shops and home builders continue the quest to create something truly unique.

1 Nothing factory remains on Barry Blomquist's C1RS, yet it's still readily recognizable as a 1962 Corvette. The Roadster Shop spent a surprisingly short nine months building the car, which shop owners Phil and Jeremy Gerber designed with artist Eric Brockmeyer. It's no surprise that this car won the 2009 Goodguys Street Machine of the Year award. *Photo © Goodguys Rod & Custom Association*

2 When Art Morrison Enterprises unveiled its 1955 Chevy 210 called *GT55*, it blew people away with its handling prowess. When *Super Chevy* tested the *GT55*, it ran 0-to-60 in 4.2 seconds, and did the quarter-mile in 12.6 seconds at 116 miles per hour. *Photo courtesy of Art Morrison Enterprises*

3 Kathy Lange wanted to drive her 1957 Thunderbird every day and fit golf bags in the trunk. Bobby Alloway built the car incorporating a plethora of subtle mods, like a stretched wheelbase, headlights that sit 1 1/2 inches lower than stock, tapered front fenders, 1955 T-Bird bumpers, and Nomad rear wheel openings. It's easy to understand why it was Goodguys' Street Machine of the Year in 2004. *Photo by Scott Killeen, courtesy of BFGoodrich*

4 Thanks to an Air Ride system and a tube frame, this Fesler Built '67 Chevy C-10 can sit a half inch off the ground. The hand-built truck is powered by an LQ4 6.0-liter Escalade engine with a Magnuson supercharger and intercooler. The smoothed ride features a Bruce Horkey's wood bed kit, 20-inch Asanti three-piece wheels, Baer brakes, and BASF paint. *Photo courtesy of Fesler Built*

5 Troy Trepanier considers this 1956 Chrysler 300B the best car Rad Rides by Troy has ever built (at least as of its debut in 2009). Rad Rides custom made the chrome-moly chassis for Nancy and Roger Ritzow's car using a Dodge Viper suspension and steering and Baer brakes. Griffin Interiors applied tan leather and Rose bird cloth to the custom bench seats. *Photo courtesy of Rad Rides by Troy*

6 The owner of this 1963 Corvette convertible had HiTek Hot Rods transform it into a "'Vette-Rod." It now rides on a chassis built by Street Shop Inc. using Art Morrison mandrel-bent perimeter rails and C4 front and rear suspension with 13-inch brakes. An LS3 crate engine sends power to a TCI 4L60E and Dana 44. *Photo ©2010 Allen Farst/ Niche Productions*

7 Denny Terzich built this 1956 Chevy, nabbing Goodguys' 2002 Street Machine of the Year award. The Tri-Five rides on a custom frame that incorporates a Fatman Fabrications front subframe with Fatman's Mustang II 2-inch dropped spindles and S&W ladder bars. The wheels are 18x8- and 20x12-inch Colorado Custom Slaters. The bulging hood covers a 572-cubic-inch big-block with a 300-horsepower Nitrous Works system. *Photo courtesy of RPM Hot Rods*

8 Bodie Stroud of BS Industries built this '60 Starliner, called *Scarliner*, which won Ford's Best of Show at the 2009 SEMA Show. It's powered by an all-aluminum DOHC supercharged 5.4-liter engine out of a 2006 Ford GT, mated to a 4R100 transmission and Strange 9-inch. The firewall had to be moved back and the car needed a new transmission tunnel.

9 "Touched By an Angel" is the theme for cancer survivor Flo Hoppe's '62 Chevy Impala SS, with its smooth sides, DuPont Hot Hues Lakeside Green paint, body line–enhancing pinstriping, and body-color Intro wheels (18x7 and 20x10). Lakeside Rods and Rides built the car. *Photo courtesy of Lakeside Rods*

10 J. R. Shaver's '56 Studebaker may look demure, but it rides on C4 Corvette suspension pieces with C4 binders and American Racing wheels. It's powered by a Bentley 6.7-liter engine with an Aston-Martin intake sporting four 2-barrel Weber carbs. The interior features European leather, Old Air A/C, and Stewart Warner gauges. A B&M shifter stirs the Turbo 400.

11 Dutchman's '57 Bel Air features a mostly stock body and chrome, with shaved door handles, a smoothed hood with airbrushed emblem, a custom grille, and the notable absence of big bumperettes. Look a little deeper, and you'll find Dutchman's new frame, a supercharged LS6, a 4L65E overdrive automatic, and Magnaflow exhaust components, topped off with DuPont Hot Hues paint. *Photo courtesy of RenovatioLucis.com*

12 Bobby Alloway built this '62 Corvette convertible for his wife, Cindy. It illustrates several Alloway's Hot Rod Shop trademarks: a nasty low stance, big rolling stock, black paint, stock body proportions, and a big engine. For the inside, Alloway swapped leather for the vinyl on a stock seat restoration kit and repro door panels. *Photo courtesy of Art Morrison Enterprises*

13 JF Kustoms (as in J. F. Launier) spent more than 11,000 hours building this '55 Chrysler wagon, called *Revolution*. Chrysler never built a two-door wagon in 1955, so JF started with a coupe and grafted on the rear lid and posts from a four-door wagon, double skinning the entire car. The color: DuPont Hot Hues Revolution yellow. *Photo courtesy of Pirelli*

14

15

16

17

14 Steve Davis, the president of Barrett-Jackson Auction Company, unveiled his '64 Fairlane resto-mod to introduce the new Planet Color Barrett-Jackson Collector Car Series line of paint. The Fairlane wears Red Hot Chili Pepper, along with polished 15-inch American Racing Torq Thrust wheels. Roush Performance built the car. *Photo courtesy of Barrett-Jackson*

15 Hulst Customs spent 3 1/2 years building this '56 Bel Air convertible for Don and Karen Blacksmith. The shop angled the windshield back 1 inch; carried the door cut lines all the way down, eliminating the rockers; Frenched the license plate into the trunk lid; and modified the rear bumper to accommodate custom exhaust tips. It also extensively modified the hood. *Photo courtesy of Hulst Customs*

16 Terry Henry built his '48 Oldsmobile back when he had a Pro Street car shop. It started out as a coupe, and then he wedge sectioned it, chopped it 5 inches, and fitted it with a lift-off top. The Olds lost its hood in place of a custom engine compartment. The front suspension came from a Chevy S-10 pickup.

17 Kirk Johnson took this '68 F-100 to Roseville Rod & Custom for a little work that snowballed into this complete redo, which won Goodguys' 2009 Truck of the Year-Late (for 1953 to 1972 models). A C6 and Currie 9-inch back up the 650-horsepower 428 Cobra Jet FE, and the stock frame has been modified. *Photo © Goodguys Rod & Custom Association*

18 GM Performance Parts created the '55 Chevy E-Rod as a proof of concept for the new GMPP E-Rod LS3 CARB-approved crate engine package. The car itself is intentionally straightforward and low buck, with styling by GM Design's Dave Ross. It wears factory-style chrome Bel Air trim, custom PPG paint, and 18-inch steel wheels from the base Camaro, with bright trim. *Photo courtesy of General Motors*

19 Ryan Brockbank describes his '61 Corvette as "vintage with an attitude." The car rides on a modified C4 chassis built by SRIII Motorsports. The LS1 engine with a Lingenfelter supercharger makes about 600 horsepower, and it's mated to a six-speed. Pearl orange and pearl white paint draw attention to the bulging Stinger hood and straight body.

20 Charlie Freeland built his '61 Impala resto-mod, now powered by a 425-horsepower 409 with a 700R4 automatic and 12-bolt Posi. He used 2-inch dropped spindles up front and 1 1/2-inch drop springs in the rear, added sway bars and power steering, and crafted his own rear wheelwells to fit the big five-spokes.

21 Jerry Crews tapped Rad Rides by Troy to build his ZL1 engine and his '66 Biscayne, nicknamed *Hurricayne*. The 540-cubic-inch aluminum big-block sports Dart heads and single-plane manifold and a 1,050cfm Holley Dominator. The car also features a Keisler Tremec TKO 600 five-speed and a 12-bolt. While the exterior is subtle, there are plenty of Troy touches. *Photo courtesy of Rad Rides by Troy*

22

23

24

22 Marquez Design used this '69 C-10 as a product development mule. It sports Marquez Design taillights, side markers, hood adjusters, and '69 Camaro turn signals integrated into the bumper, plus the first set of preproduction one-piece door panels. The distinctive wheels are Boze Pro Touring models, and the truck looks more modern thanks to Brothers one-piece glass, shaved side trim, and a body-color front bumper. *Photo courtesy of Marquez Design*

23 Steve's Restorations & Hot Rods applied a two-tone design to Brittany Busa's attention-getting '56 Bel Air using PPG Vibrance Yella and Performance Yellow paint, a tri-coat system with base-coat colors and PPG's Emberglo midcoat. The shoebox runs a 350 built by Bill Battle and Lynde Schultz, a TCI Street Fighter Turbo 350 with 3,000-stall converter, a line lock, and Foose Nitrous II wheels. *Photo courtesy of Steve's Restorations*

24 Howard Brook and Performance West Group transformed Larry Weiner's '59 Biscayne sedan delivery into the *Chevrolet Winged Express*. It's powered by a 700-horsepower Turn Key Engine Supply LS2 with Turn Key engine management and wiring systems, a Kenne Bell 2.4L twin-screw supercharger and air-to-water intercooler, Air Flow Research heads, Comp Cams 'stick, and Turn Key headers. *Photo courtesy of Performance West Group*

25 At first glance, it may look more show than go, but the 600-cubic-inch big-block Ford in the *SR61* throws down 920 horsepower and 810 lb-ft of torque. Body mods include shaved emblems, door handles, fuel filler, hood trim and vent windows, brass side molding, airbrushed roofline stars, smoothed bumpers, chromed grille and headlight buckets, and side-exit exhaust. *Photo © Summit Racing Equipment*

26 Lakeside Rods built this '59 Corvette called *Evolution* for Garland Miller. The incredibly sleek ride features custom rear bumpers and taillights, custom center-exit exhaust, and a stock windshield with polished edges that Lakeside Rods sunk down into the cowl a few inches. It's powered by a 572-horsepower 385 that Faerman Racing Engines built. *Photo courtesy of Lakeside Rods*

27 The K&N Engineering Race Shop built this '55 Chevy 210. The only aluminum on the car surrounds the Panasonic head unit in the original dash. K&N even powder-coated the Lokar gas pedal black for a more factory look. Santini Paint & Body applied the House of Kolor Platinum and Sunset paint, and Ron Mangus stitched up matching upholstery for the factory bench seats. *Photo courtesy of K&N*

28 Fesler transformed this '69 Blazer from a 4x4 into a '30s-inspired roadster in a little more than four months. The shop cut the windshield 4 inches and laid it back 5 degrees, cut down the doors, attached the Goodmark cowl hood with custom hinges, and installed a Sir Michaels roll pan. *Photo courtesy of Fesler Built*

25

26

27

28

29

29 Barry's Speed Shop/SRRC built Don Carlile's '62 Biscayne, named *Hurricayne*. It features a Magnuson supercharger atop the 6.0-liter engine, Bassett headers, Mattson radiator, a great stance with QA1 coil-overs, a one-off grille, a super-straight body, and impressive paintwork by Tony Correia's Speed Shop Custom Paint.

30

30 Jay Leno took the resto-mod concept to a whole 'nother level when he unveiled this 1,070-horsepower twin-turbo '66 Olds Toronado. Leno's *Big Dog Garage* maintained a surprisingly stock look, right down to the Trumpet Gold color (albeit done in BASF base coat/clear coat). The formerly front-drive car now rides on a modified C5 Corvette chassis and suspension. *Photo courtesy of General Motors*

31

31 HiTek Hot Rods' '57 Bel Air has a retro, mostly original look inside and out. This Chevy not only rides on an Art Morrison GMax chassis, it's powered by an LS7 with a cool ram air system that uses the fresh air ducts above the headlights to route cold air to a custom airbox. *Photo courtesy of HiTek Hot Rods*

32

32 Roy Brizio's '55 Chevy 210 demonstrates the "less is more" aesthetic he usually applies to '32 Fords. Thom Taylor did the rendering with a subtle '60s Corvette theme, including a Corvette steering wheel and one-off 17x8 and 18x10 Billet Specialties wheels reminiscent of '62 Vette wheel covers. Brizio smoothed, peaked, and louvered the hood and added a custom grille to the Danchuk surround. *Photo courtesy of Art Morrison Enterprises*

33 When Art Morrison Enterprises wanted to develop a new chassis for the C1 incorporating C5 and C6 components, *Popular Hot Rodding* got on board to make this a project car. Its *3G* name comes from the project's goal: to make at least 1g of performance in the lateral axis, acceleration, and deceleration, which it did, averaging 1.05g on the skid pad. *Photo courtesy of Art Morrison Enterprises*

34 Steve Luethge's totally traditional '56 Chevy features a stock body and a low look, thanks to Air Ride Technologies. Lakeside Rods outfitted the two-door sedan with a built 355-cubic-inch small-block, Turbo 350 and Ford 9-inch, aluminized exhaust and Flowmaster mufflers. There are some subtle mods to the body, like custom stainless side trim that eliminates the two-tone spear. *Photo courtesy of Lakeside Rods*

35 Jeff Romig, general manager of supercharger and performance products for Eaton Corporation, had Classic Automotive Restoration Specialists (CARS Inc.) build this '51 Chevy. CARS Inc. boxed the frame and upgraded it with a Fatman Fabrications Mustang II IFS, Eaton Detroit Springs' 2-inch lowering leaf springs, and a Moser Engineering 12-bolt with an Eaton Posi. *Photo courtesy of CARS Inc.*

Chapter 2
Muscle Cars

The caliber of muscle cars being built these days is absolutely mind-blowing. They look incredible. The proportions are stunning. The fit and finish is exquisite. They're quick and fast. They stop far better than they did when they were new— and far better than plenty of new cars too. And some of them even handle as well as Ferraris.

The cars in this chapter do represent the breadth of the hobby.

There are serious g-machines, along with Pro Street cars and resto-mods. There are strikingly modern-looking rides and heartwarmingly nostalgic cars. There are fat-wallet race cars that happen to be streetable and budget buildups that make fine auto-crossers or bracket racers. In short, I have to believe there's something here to inspire just about anybody.

1 This '67 Camaro definitely takes the prize for biggest hood bulge and most pronounced use of a cold-air intake—and it definitely elevates Pro Street to a new stratum. ProRides/RPM built the car for company owner Denny Terzich, and it doesn't just look nasty—its 580-cubic-inch engine with a ProCharger F3 and blow-through carb produces a whomping 1,500-plus rear-wheel horsepower, good for 7.76-second ETs. *Photo courtesy of RPM Hot Rods*

2 John Hotchkis of Hotchkis Performance noticed there weren't many Mopars competing in autocross events, so he built the E-Max 1970 Challenger. The E-Max sports a 340 Six Pack, Tremec TKO 600 five-speed, Hurst Sidewinder-shifter, Chrysler 8 3/4 limited-slip rear, Flaming River quick-ratio steering, StopTech brakes, and Forgeline 18-inch ZX3P wheels with Yokohama Neova ZR tires. *Photo courtesy of Hotchkis*

3 Jim Wangers (aka the Godfather of the GTO) lent his name and support to Big 3 Performance, which created the now 1-of-1 Jim Wangers Signature Edition GTO (originally intended for limited production). The body is from 1969, but everything else is new, including a Roadster Shop chassis fitted with Detroit Speed C6 front suspension, triangulated four-bar rear suspension, and Jim Wangers Signature Wilwood brakes. *Photo courtesy of Jim Wangers*

4 Scott Taylor's *Naja* Mustang rides on an Art Morrison MaxG chassis with Air Ride RidePro suspension. FE Specialties built the engine, starting with a Shelby aluminum 427 block (now 490 cubic inches) and porting the Edelbrock aluminum heads. It makes 705 horsepower on pure engine, and Mike Thermos at Nitrous Supply plumbed it for a 200-horsepower Pro Shot Fogger system. *Photo courtesy of Scott Taylor*

2

3

4

5

6

7

8

5 Gary Abraham told Rad Rides by Troy that he wanted a '70 Nova with a massive engine, a nice interior, and a gray paint job, like the car he had as a teenager. The result: *Notorious*, Goodguys' 2008 Muscle Machine of the Year. The car takes some styling cues from the '69 Camaro, including the front valance. *Photo courtesy of Rad Rides by Troy*

6 Tom McBride of Bowler Transmission drove the 408 Windsor-powered '70 Fastlane Fairlane to a ninth-place finish in the 2009 Optima Batteries Ultimate Street Car Invitational— after driving it the 2,000 miles from Illinois to Nevada. Tom swapped in a four-link rear suspension, coil-overs up front, a new rack-and-pinion, and custom-made strut tower braces, with help from the folks at Air Ride. *Photo courtesy of Steven Rupp*

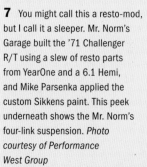

7 You might call this a resto-mod, but I call it a sleeper. Mr. Norm's Garage built the '71 Challenger R/T using a slew of resto parts from YearOne and a 6.1 Hemi, and Mike Parsenka applied the custom Sikkens paint. This peek underneath shows the Mr. Norm's four-link suspension. *Photo courtesy of Performance West Group*

8 Johnson's Hot Rod Shop built Nathan Powell's '69 Camaro, which features a hydroformed subframe, an interior by Paul Atkins, tucked-in bumpers, and Glasurit two-stage paint. The 540-cubic-inch big-block Chevy with Dart heads makes 700 horsepower, and it's linked to a six-speed manual transmission. *Photo © Goodguys Rod & Custom Association*

9 Patrick Nance of D & P Classic Chevy's '71 Chevelle, *Full Yella Jacket*, features shaved door handles, badges and trim, and blacked-out bumpers. He added a bit of low-key shine with the Strut grille, lighting, and U.S. Wheels (19x8 and 20x9.5 with 245/40-19 and 285/35-20 BFGoodrich tires). *Photo courtesy of Strut*

10 Ringbrothers split the rear window and custom machined more than 70 parts—including the side vents, gas cap, taillight bezels, and exhaust tip/diffuser—for Doug Hoppes' *Reactor* '67 Mustang, which won the Mothers Shine award, a Ford design award at the SEMA Show, and Goodguys' 2007 Street Machine of the Year. *Photo © Goodguys Rod & Custom Association*

11 Street Concepts' *Beast* '71 Challenger is powered by a Mopar 540-cubic-inch all-aluminum Hemi mated to a Jet 727 transmission with Gear Vendors under/overdrive and a Speedway Engineering quick-change rear end. The car features a Magnumforce tubular front suspension, QA1 coil-overs, SWS four-link, Baer brakes, Redline Gauge Works dash with Stewart Warner gauges, Cobra seats, and Street Concepts' trademark suede interior. *Photo courtesy of Street Concepts*

9

10

11

12

12 Time Machines outfitted the '68 *Bullseye* Dart with a 500-plus-horsepower 5.7-liter Hemi with Imagine electronic stack injection and FAST engine management. The car also runs a Hurst shifter, Passon A835 overdrive, and McLeod clutch. The smooth, clean body sports Stephens Performance bumpers, a custom hood scoop, and PPG Deep Black paint, with 18x7 and 18x10 Halibrand Kidney Bean 5 wheels. *Photo courtesy of Performance West Group*

13 When the producers of *Gone in 60 Seconds* wanted a shop to build turnkey *Eleanor* Mustangs, they tapped Classic Recreations. This 100 percent new "1967" is available with two different versions of the Keith Craft Racing 410-cubic-inch FI 351W stroker engine, making either 535 or 770 horsepower. *Photo courtesy of Classic Recreations*

13

14 What do you get when you cross a Pro Street car with a mini-truck and a lowrider? Akira Yamamoto's '67 Camaro, which was built by Hot Style Customs in Akira's hometown of Kyoto, Japan. The Roots-style blower sits atop a 383-cubic-inch small-block. It features Universal Air suspension, a custom dash with Dakota Digital gauges, flamed upholstery, and 20-inch Work LS 105 wheels all the way around.

15 YearOne's Ghostworks Garage took the second Promax '67 Chevy II replica ever made and built it into this car on the TV show *Rides*. Starting with a bare shell meant the garage spent lots of time working out things like glass, weather stripping, electricals, and an interior, though it did come with a prefabbed dash. *Photo courtesy of YearOne, all rights reserved*

16 Grand Touring Garage built the street-legal *Trans-Cammer* '70 Mustang so it would be capable of serious high-speed competition. The rear undercarriage has flat floor panels, and the rear bulkhead air panels and diffuser strakes assist with aerodynamics. The Mustang won the 2009 Sony PlayStation Gran Turismo Best of Show award at SEMA. *Photo courtesy of Grand Touring Garage*

Chevelle Scope Creep

The folks at The Roadster Shop bought both of these cars for research and development purposes so they could develop a Chevelle chassis to be sold by sister company RS Performance. First they got the '66 to create a chassis for 1964 to 1967 models and then the '70 to make a 1968 to 1972 version. But both cars quickly morphed from R&D mules into full-on project cars.

The '66 received a Bill Mitchell Hardcore Racing aluminum 540-cubic-inch big-block making 685 horsepower and 685 lb-ft of torque, which was mated to a 4L65E semi-auto transmission with Master Control paddle shifters and Ford 9-inch. The new RS chassis was outfitted with Afco remote-reservoir double-adjustable coil-overs up front and QA1 adjustable coil-overs rear, Wilwood 14-inch drilled and slotted rotors, 19x9- and 20x12-inch Boze wheels, and Michelin Pilot Sport SP2 255/35R19 and 335/30R20 tires.

The '70 is definitely distinctive, with its Porsche GT3 RS green paint. It features a 640-horsepower Turn Key Performance LS7, Viper-spec Tremec T56 six-speed, and 9-inch with 3.70:1 gears. Obviously, it rides on an RS chassis, this time with Eibach springs and Penske shocks, as well as 18x10 and 19x12 Forgeline wheels wrapped in 275/35R18 and 345/35R19 Michelin Pilot Sport PS2s.

Super Chevy magazine put both cars through their paces on a skid pad, and both pulled an impressive .98g.

Photo courtesy of The Roadster Shop

17 Mike Schmaltz built his '65 Malibu SS, which sports a 454-cubic-inch big-block topped with an Edelbrock Performer RPM Airgap intake and Demon 750 carb. Schmaltz also chose an MSD 6AL ignition and distributor, Flowmaster American Thunder 2 1/2-inch exhaust, and 700R4 overdrive automatic. Mr. D's Custom Auto Painting applied the traditional flamed paint. *Photo courtesy of Hedman Hedders*

18 Gearhead Garage treated this '68 Camaro RS/SS convertible to a resto-mod build. While it appears mostly stock, the trunk houses a serious sound system, and the hood tops a 670-horsepower LS2 with a MagnaCharger. It's mated to a Tremec five-speed, and a Hotchkis suspension seriously improves handling. *Photo courtesy of Gearhead Garage*

19

20

21

19 Starting with a '70 Plymouth Satellite, YearOne created this "NASCAR Superbird for the street" for celebrity Bill Goldberg. It features mostly period-correct NASCAR-style mods, but with coil spring suspension and a full roll cage. Evernham Motorsports contributed the NASCAR-spec 358-cubic-inch Dodge engine. *Photo courtesy of YearOne, all rights reserved*

20 It took approximately $1.3 million and three years for Autoworks International to build Steve Groat's *Obsidian SG-One* '67 Mustang, with its 847-horsepower twin-supercharged EFI engine, Formula 1–style paddle shifters, extensive body mods, California Mustang smoked glass, tubular frame, four-point hidden roll cage, RRS coil-over suspension, and removable aluminum belly pan. *Photo by Nick Nacca, courtesy of ScoCar*

21 Lakeside Rods and Rides built Dave and Karen Leisinger's '67 Camaro, which rides on a full chassis with Detroit Speed suspension front and rear, a 9-inch Ford rear end, Wilwood brakes, and 18x8 and 20x12 Billet Specialties wheels wrapped in Michelin tires. Check out the custom taillights. *Photo courtesy of Lakeside Rods*

22 Many of the street machines in this book are high-dollar rides, but not this one. Pete Martinez has about $15,000 invested in his '72 Nova, which just so happens to pull .97g on the skid pad. It's powered by a 350 small-block with a Barry Grant Mighty Demon 650 carb and MSD electronic distributor, mated to a Turbo 400. *Photo courtesy of Hotchkis*

23 Amazingly enough, Bryan Frank started with one of just nine convertible Trans Ams made in 1969. RPM Hot Rods transformed it into the 2009 Goodguys/Detroit Speed Muscle Machine of the Year by adding extended rockers, a blended Camaro/Firebird front valance, a reworked Fatman front subframe, a modified Detroit Speed QuadraLink, and Air Ride Shockwaves. *Photo © Goodguys Rod & Custom Association*

24

24 Cam Douglass of Optima Batteries originally built this '71 Z28 as a Silver State Classic competitor. Amir Rosenbaum, the owner of Spectre Performance, has since bought the car and updated it. The injected LT1 block is connected to a six-speed, and the car sports a Hotchkis TVS suspension, big Wilwood brakes with front/rear bias control, and American Racing wheels. *Photo courtesy of Spectre*

25

25 Foose Design turned a 1970 Barracuda into the *Terracuda* for Darren Metropolis. In classic Foose fashion, Chip reproportioned the car, changing every body panel. He clay modeled the interior, coming up with a racy, yet luxurious design that uses Cobra seats and Ferrari leather. Under the hood: a Mopar 6.4-liter Hemi tied to a Tremec five-speed and Ford 9-inch. *Photo by Ryan Hagel, courtesy of Pirelli*

26

26 Modern Muscle builds '69 and '70 fastback Mustangs for customers that feature classic Mustang sheet metal and a modern Mustang GT500 KR–style drivetrain. These Mustangs come with a 9-inch Ford rear with buyer's choice of gears, a Ford Racing Hurst shifter, a FAST engine management system, and SSBC disc brakes all around. *Photo courtesy of Performance West Group*

27 Plum Floored Creations' *Dark Runner* is powered by a Generation III Hemi that now displaces the magic 426 cubic inches (7.0 liters). It features forged internals with Wiseco dished pistons, a Custom Aluminum Radiators four-core unit with twin 15-inch SPAL electric fans, and Gibson 3-inch exhaust with an X-pipe, which exits through the rockers. The paint is Planet Color Obsidian Black. *Photo courtesy of Plum Floored Creations*

28 Ya gotta love a hot Buick. RideTech's '70 GSX is powered by a 538-horsepower, 455-cubic-inch Stage 1 Buick engine with TA Performance Street Eliminator aluminum heads, SPX intake, and BigStuff 3 EFI. Of course it has an Air Ride air suspension—the Street Challenge package—along with Fatman Fabrications G-Max spindles. *Photo courtesy of RideTech*

29

30

31a

29 Body shop owner Roy Pigford did 99 percent of the work on his '66 Chevy Nova, which was Goodguys' 2005 Street Machine of the Year. If the proportions look a little different, that's because he chopped 2 inches off the top and moved the front axle forward 2 inches and the rear 3 inches. *Photo © Goodguys Rod & Custom Association*

30 This '69 Mustang has the Galpin Auto Sports look, with PPG Green Pearl Chartreuse paint on the Dynacorn body shell and a 525-horsepower Ford Racing 351 with Hilborn injection peeking through the hood. Amazingly, it was assembled in less than 24 hours on-stage in the Ford booth during the 2009 SEMA Show, starting with an engine on a stand and piles of parts. *Photo courtesy of Galpin Auto Sports*

31a Steven Rupp's Bad Penny 1968 Camaro won the 2008 Optima Batteries Ultimate Street Car Invitational. Its 402-cubic-inch LS2 makes 561 horsepower, and the chassis features a 21st Century Street Machines front subframe with C5 control arms and spindles, along with a Lateral Dynamics three-link with a Watt's link in the rear. The Anvil Auto carbon fiber hood weighs just 17 pounds. *Photo courtesy of Steven Rupp*

31 Car owner Larry Olsen teamed up with Jeff Roling Classic Auto to build this '66 Chevy II, which was smoothed and then fitted with a cowl-style hood and custom grille. The car features a 565-horsepower LS7, 4L60E automatic transmission, Chris Alston's Chassisworks front subframe, Heidt's Superide IRS, and custom Recovery Room seats swathed in red leather. *Photo by Josh Mishler, courtesy of Recovery Room*

32 Hill's Hot Rods spent about 1,800 hours building Bob Brandt's '70 Challenger, which has a plethora of subtle mods. Most notable is the use of a grille, headlights, and taillights from a 2009 Challenger. Brandt built his own 850-horspower, 540-inch Hemi. Hill's applied the House of Kolor and PPG paint and graphics.

33 RPM Hot Rods built this '72 Chevelle for Pittsburgh Steeler Kendall Simmons. The team started with body panels from Goodmark and then fabricated the grille, reworked the rain gutters, massaged the bumpers, and spent countless hours on the hood. The 454-powered A-body rides on an Art Morrison chassis with Wilwood brakes, Billet Specialties Roulette wheels, and 245/30-20 and 285/35-22 BFGoodrich G-Force T/A tires. *Photo © Goodguys Rod & Custom Association*

34

35

36

34 Devan Glissmeyer tapped Kindig-it Design to turn his '68 Mustang fastback into a smooth, sleek car that could be driven. Extensive body mods include the bumpers, hood (with '69 shaker scoop), headlight buckets, wheel arches, fender flares, sail panels, and quarter windows. The sizable 14.5-inch Wilwood rotors are to scale with the 20- and 24x15-inch Intro Custom wheels.
Photo © Goodguys Rod & Custom Association

35 Modern Muscle cleaned up the look of this '71 Cuda with its shaved door handles, locks, side marker lights, mirrors, and trim. Pinstriping in '70 Cuda Limelight green separates the DuPont Standox custom silver and Real Black paint and makes the Hemi billboard really pop.
Photo courtesy of Performance West Group

36 This '70 Chevelle SS resto-mod looks remarkably stock, thanks to YearOne interior parts and Goodmark body panels. Then you spot the Baer brakes through the Budnik wheels. Fesler Built modified the car, installing a GM Ram Jet fuel-injected 454, Magnaflow stainless-steel exhaust, 4L80E trans, Hotchkis suspension, and Vintage Air air conditioning.
Photo courtesy of Fesler Built

37 The new Baldwin-Motion delivered its first '69 Phase III Camaro to Dave Flynn. The turnkey street machine features a 565-cubic-inch, 700-horsepower aluminum big-block, and Tremec TKO 600 five-speed. The Motion Red ride has been mini-tubbed and outfitted with subframe connectors, a Motion independent rear suspension, and a tubular front suspension. *Photo courtesy of Baldwin-Motion*

38 Johnson's Hot Rod Shop tweaked every part of this '71 Barracuda for Bob Johnson (no relation), who wanted a car that could run 200 miles per hour and still be streetable. The 572-cubic-inch Hemi sits behind the front axle centerline in the tube chassis, which features C5 Corvette suspension components. It won Goodguys' 2006 Street Machine of the Year award. *Photo © Goodguys Rod & Custom Association*

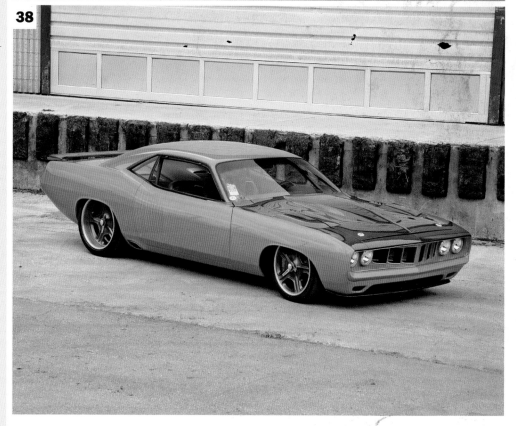

39

39 Lakeside Rods and Rides built Kevin and Karen Alstott's '68 Camaro with black and copper styling. The mini-tubbed, small-block car sports a TCI 700R trans, 9-inch Ford limited-slip rear, Detroit Speed and Engineering suspension, subframe connectors, and big Baer brakes—enabling it to win Goodguys' autocross at Columbus and putting it into the top-five contenders for 2009 Street Machine of the Year. *Photo courtesy of Lakeside Rods*

40

40 The Roadster Shop built this '70 Chevelle convertible for Ted Hellard, who wanted a serious-handling resto-mod. The car looks mostly stock outside, except for the Goodmark hood and the sectioned, narrowed, and close-set bumpers. The paint scheme obviously is not stock, from the black bumpers to the PPG Chili Red color, and the custom-mixed graphite stripes are covered in matte clear coat. *Photo courtesy of The Roadster Shop*

41 YearOne built *Blackened*, a '69 Mach 1 Mustang, for Bud Brutsman (producer of TV shows like *Rides*, *Overhaulin'*, and *Hot Rod TV*). The modernized Mustang sports a supercharged 4.6-liter from a 2003 Cobra and a Metco Motorsports front pulley system to pump up the boost. Gloss-black Foose wheels with polished aluminum outers provide a bit of brightwork on the exterior. *Photo courtesy of BFGoodrich*

42 Precision Coachworks (sister company of RideTech/Air Ride) built the 1970 *SuperNova*, which was Goodguys' 2009 giveaway car. It's backed by a 615-horsepower World Products LS 427 with a Vintage Air FrontRunner setup, Dynatech headers, and Flowmaster exhaust. The Bowler 4L65E transmission can be controlled by Twist Machine paddle shifters. *Photo courtesy of RideTech*

41

42

43

43 Tommy Vieth had always wanted a Pro Street car, so that's the route he took with his '68 Camaro. The Kim Barr Racing Engines 498-cubic-inch Chevy mill features JE pistons, Dart Pro 1 355 aluminum heads, a Mooneyham 8-71 blower with Chuck Newton 1050 Dominator carbs, MSD Ignition, and Lemons headers with Spin Tech 4-inch exhaust. It makes 910 horsepower and 740 lb-ft of torque at 6,400 rpm. *Photo by DreamCars.com*

44 Brett Hunter of Hunter Body Shop, Customs & Hot Rods built his '70 6.1-liter Hemi 'Cuda with lowered rocker panels, custom valances, flush-mounted glass and shaved side markers, drip rails, and locks. The Mopar also features a YearOne hood, a hand-built grille, Air Ride's Street Challenge suspension, subframe connectors, and Bonspeed 19x8- and 22x10-inch wheels. *Photo © Goodguys Rod & Custom Association*

44

45 Top Line Performance performed a rotisserie resto-mod on Jim Wilke's '66 Chevelle Malibu, adding a Super Sport hood, ZZ502 crate engine, Flowmaster 3-inch exhaust, Richmond five-speed, 12-bolt Posi with 3.08 gears, Hotchkis Sport suspension package, Baer brakes with drilled and slotted rotors, and Billet Specialties wheels. *Photo courtesy of Jim Wilke*

46 Guitar legend Kenny Wayne Shepherd wanted a Duster because that's the car his mom drove when his parents met. His friend Ted Moser of Picture Car Warehouse, which specializes in building movie cars, helped clean up this '70 model. He applied the dark graphite over Saab frost green metallic paint, and Chip Foose handled the hood graphics. *Photo courtesy of YearOne, all rights reserved*

47

48

47 Mary Pozzi has won 11 SCCA national autocross championships, and now she's dominating the street machine autocross scene with her '73 Camaro RS. Mary believes the second-generation F-body offers superior weight distribution and a stiffer platform than the more popular early cars. She runs a GM Fast Burn 385 and a Tremec TKO five-speed. *Photo courtesy of Hotchkis*

48 To make Tom Boldry's '69 Hemi-powered Charger look more aggressive, Rock's Rod & Custom modified every body panel except the roof. The stock grille sits in a custom surround over a custom apron and chin spoiler, and the fabbed bumper flows into the fenders. Rock's shaved the door handles and locks and put a bow in the hood and cowl. *Photo © Goodguys Rod & Custom Association*

49 Modern Muscle's Pro Touring '69 Camaro rides on an Art Morrison chassis, and it's powered by a 650-horsepower stack-injected big-block mated to a TKO 600 and C5 Corvette differential. The shop also chopped the convertible top and finished the car off with DuPont Standox paint and graphics that accentuate the bulging hood. *Photo courtesy of Performance West Group*

50 Spectre Performance fabricated the aluminum SpeedSplitter on the front of its 1970 El Camino. The rest of the car was built by Jimmy Shine of So-Cal Speed Shop and his team on the TV show *Hard Shine*. The goal: make the front/mid-engine car faster than a 512TR Ferrari on a racetrack. *Photo courtesy of Spectre*

49

50

Chapter 3
Modern Street Machines

The new Camaro and Challenger have inspired a flurry of street machine building activity. And the Mustang has been a perennial street machine favorite pretty much since the Fox-body car debuted.

Still, there has been a noticeable lapse in interest in most vehicles from the late 1970s, 1980s, and 1990s. However, I suspect that's about to change, as the trendsetters start paying more attention to these cars and trucks. Case in point: Rad Rides by Troy is working on an '87 Camaro right now.

This chapter includes a fun assortment of home-built and high-end machinery. There are plenty of cool one-offs, but there are also quite a few turnkey street machines. That shouldn't be too much of a surprise, considering it is a lot easier to go into production when you start with vehicles that are readily available.

1 After being in a helicopter accident while serving as a Marine, Mouse Prosen underwent 18 major surgeries. He built this 2006 Mustang GT called *Saphira* as a sort of therapy. It features a 900-horsepower Granatelli Motorsports–built 302, with a Paxton Novi 2200 supercharger, Granatelli 1G suspension, Liquid Metal wheels, CDC Glassback roof, Cervini Stalker hood, and Agent 47 mirrors. *Photo by Peter Linney, courtesy of ScoCar*

2 The 2009 Dodge Challenger Targa started out as a Mopar Challenger drag race package car, which got heavily modified to compete in the 2,200-kilometer Targa Newfoundland road rally. The chin spoiler was developed in a wind tunnel to reduce lift. The Snakeskin Green paint is a Dodge Viper color. *Photo courtesy of Chrysler*

3 Jared Martin built his 2003 Dodge Ram SLT, stuffing a 426-cubic-inch Arrington crate engine under the hood and juicing it with a Zex Hemi 75-100-125-150-horsepower wet kit. The nitrous system's dual purge setup exits through the Proglass shaker inlets. Of course, Jared runs Royal Purple synthetic lubricants throughout, since he works in the company's sales department. *Photo courtesy of Royal Purple*

4 Fesler Built has teamed up with Chevrolet legend Jon Moss to produce a limited run of 2010 Fesler-Moss Camaros. There are three variations, and this is the top dog, with a supercharged LS9 and a full Pedders Race suspension. Fesler will even build a matching '69 Camaro with the same engine and performance as the 2010. *Photo courtesy of Fesler Built*

5 Richard Petty has shifted gears, from building NASCAR racers to street machines. This 2009 Challenger, the first car produced by Petty's Garage, was completely disassembled and placed on a rotisserie so it could be painted the trademark Petty Blue by BASF. It's now powered by a 585-horsepower Arrington Engines Gen III 426 Hemi. *Photo courtesy of Petty's Garage*

6 Katech's ClubSport package for the Z06 Corvette reduces curb weight to 2,915 pounds while improving grip, cornering, braking, and downforce. The Exedy twin-disc clutch reduces drivetrain mass and makes for easy rev-matched downshifts, and the 18-gauge stainless Katech exhaust features an X-pipe, two lightweight mufflers, over-axle pipes, and Corsa quad tips to shave pounds and produce a deep tone. *Photo courtesy of Katech Performance.*

7 Berger Chevrolet and GMMG teamed up to build about 30 Dick Harrell Edition 2003 Camaros in 2005 and 2006. Suspension mods include Eibach lowering springs, rear lower control arm relocation brackets, and GMMG subframe connectors and front sway bar. They offered three power levels, ranging from an LS6 to this 630-horsepower 427 Phase III setup. *Photo courtesy of Hotchkis*

8 Gordon Heidacker was a senior-level executive at Chrysler and AMC for 23 years, part of the initial Viper team, and founder of Chrysler's internal Skunkwerks. Now he's founded Heide Performance Products, which developed this new Challenger-based Daytona, and Mopar plans to sell many of the styling pieces. This car combines styling cues from the original Dodge Daytona and the Plymouth Superbird. *Photo courtesy of Heide Performance Products*

9 CGS Motorsports built the 540-horsepower FlatBack 2010 Mustang, designed by Sean Smith of SS Designs. The gloss-black graphics are actually the car's original color, while the matte gray metallic paint is from BASF. It sports 22-inch one-off Colorado Custom wheels, Roush body kit, CGS exhaust and air intake, Eibach coil-over suspension and sway bars, Whipple supercharger, Baer brakes, and Pecca leather on Recaro seats.

Dueling Mustangs

Summit's orange '95 Mustang GT is called *5.0 Revival*, since the '95 model was the last of the original 5.0-liter cars. But this one has been bored and stroked from 302 to 347-cubic-inches by Fox Lake and fitted with a Summit Racing 347 rotating kit. It features Trick Flow Twisted Wedge aluminum heads, Track Max roller cam, Track Heat EFI manifold, and 1.6:1 roller rockers, good for 311 rear-wheel horsepower. The Summit parts list includes shorty headers, off-road H-pipe, cat-back exhaust, 1 1/2-inch lowering springs, rear control arm kit, and Summit Extreme slotted and cross-drilled brake rotors. The 18-inch American Racing Killer wheels feature a black powder-coat finish with a stainless-steel lip, and they're shod in BFG g-Force T/A KDW tires.

Summit's other '95 Mustang GT couldn't be more different. It started out as a parts-development mule. When that life was over, the shop stripped it down and sent it to Tim McAmis Race cars to get an eight-point roll cage, subframe connectors, and 14-inch mini-tubs. *QuikStang* may have been built back in 1999, but the 1,000-horsepower drop top still attracts a crowd at events. The suspension features a Griggs Racing tubular front K-member and A-arms, rear trailing arms with an adjustable panhard bar and torque arm, plus Granatelli sway bars, Koni coil-overs, Baer Pro Race brakes, 18-inch Wheel Vintiques Billet Mach I rims, and Kumho Ecsta tires. Euro-Body attached the Cervini body kit and cowl hood and the Saleen Speedster tonneau cover and then squirted the Lexus Bright Ivy Pearl paint. Dean Blum, the man in charge of project cars for Summit, coined the term Pro Millenium to describe *QuikStang* and its ilk, meaning a late-model body style with a big-inch engine, a power adder, EFI, and big meats. *Photos © Summit Racing Equipment*

10

11

12

10 Mark Abate of Sound Choice Audio and Performance had hoped to get a 2010 Camaro SS to build for the 2009 SEMA Show, but GM surprised him with a V-6. So he bolted on two turbos and made about 550 horsepower. The car, called *Heritage*, sports a custom wide-body kit, 22-inch iForged wheels, and AP Racing brakes. *Photo by Derek Schimanke, courtesy of SCAP*

11 Tom Velez updated the handling on his 1980 Trans Am (right) with Hotchkis subframe connectors, adjustable tubular front and rear sway bars, sport springs, tie rod sleeves, and geometry-corrected tubular upper and lower A-arms. Steve Strope of Pure Vision Design built the 2003 Trans Am WS6 for his wife, Allison, with Hotchkis TVS suspension, a custom "chicken" adapted from a 1980 T/A kit, and YearOne billet Lace wheels. *Photo courtesy of Hotchkis*

12 George Huisman, CEO of Classic Design Concepts, swapped a 2003 Cobra powertrain into his '03 Mach 1 Mustang. The supercharged 4.6-liter/T56 six-speed swap was not as easy as you might expect; it required changing the three main body electrical harnesses, the EEC V processor, and the fuel tank. With a Lightning blower pulley for more boost, it makes 525 horsepower. *Photo courtesy of Classic Design Concepts*

13 Jeffrey's Custom Conversions builds these Super Street Series cars that look remarkably like NASCAR Sprint Cup cars but are fully streetable, street-legal, and even equipped with A/C and a stereo. Jeffrey's design team will formulate graphics to suit—all for a fraction of the cost of actual stock car sponsorship. *Photo courtesy of Jeffrey's Custom Conversions*

14 NASCAR powerhouse Hendrick Motorsports commissioned Callaway Cars to develop and build a run of Hendrick Motorsports 25th Anniversary 2010 Camaro SSs. Callaway's Eaton TVS series supercharger, high-flow air intake and exhaust, and engine management recalibration increase power from 426 to 582 ponies. They report ETs of 11.89 seconds at 120.1 miles per hour and 3.9-second 0-to-60 times. *Photo courtesy of Callaway Cars*

15 Rick Bottom Designs created the *2Go* 2010 Camaro in conjunction with Razzi GFX and Modern Muscle. The car makes a mind-bending 1,000 horsepower on 93-octane pump gas—and runs 9-second ETs—thanks to a Labonte ISG-S3 water methanol injection system. The attention-getting styling includes a Razzi/Rick Bottom Signature four-piece body kit, MPD cowl induction hood and spoiler, Carriage Works billet grilles, Defender Worx side gill trim, and BASF paint.

16

16 Mr. Norm's 2008 Super Challenger draws inspiration from the 1970 Challenger T/A. The company will outfit any new Challenger SRT8 with graphics, interior dress-up goodies, and a plethora of options, including the front spoiler overlay on this 2008. Performance upgrades include a supercharger, intercooler, Kenne Bell ram air system and Optimizer II engine management system, and Corsa cat-back exhaust. *Photo courtesy of Performance West Group*

17

17 J. R. Granatelli built his 2005 Mustang as an R&D/demo vehicle for Granatelli Motorsports, hence the attention-getting paint and Pro Stock–style wing. The *Turbo Terror* boasts his single turbo kit, which includes a 76mm Turbonetics turbocharger, Tial wastegate, Granatelli compressor bypass valve, two Spearco intercoolers, a 2.5-inch downpipe, and a high-flow twin-cat system leading into a Granatelli 3-inch cat-back exhaust. *Photo by Drew Phillips, courtesy of Granatelli Motorsports*

18 Patrick Burris outfitted his 2000 GMC with Denali headlights, a billet grille, Street Scene mirrors, a SnugTop tonneau cover, Sir Michaels roll pan, DJM 6-inch rear flip kit, 4-inch lowering A-arms up front, Auto Meter gauges, and Centerline Stingray III 20x8 and 22x8.5 wheels with Toyo tires. The GMPP LSX block features a Lunati crank and rods, Diamond pistons, Crane cam, and Dart heads. *Photo courtesy of Royal Purple*

19 Lingenfelter's concept TA may be based on the 2010 Camaro, but it was inspired by the '71 Pontiac Trans Am. I think they really nailed it, from the classic paint job and front fascia to the metal-turned instrument panel and honeycomb wheels (20-inchers wrapped in Nitto rubber). It's even powered by a 455-cubic-inch engine, though it's not a Pontiac block.

18

19

20 Dan Kahn built his budget '99 Camaro SS. He installed a ported throttle body with a coolant bypass, an LS6 intake manifold, a Volant cold air intake, and Kooks headers, and swapped the 4L60E auto for a T56 manual with a Centerforce clutch. He also opted for Corbeau A4 seats and a billet grille from 6LiterEater Designs. *Photo courtesy of Hotchkis*

21 Trent's Trick Upholstery created *Project Stunner,* a 2010 Camaro SS with butterscotch and Chevy blue BASF paint. The amber LED halos pick up the butterscotch, and the car also has Lightwerkz HID headlights and LED taillights. On the performance front, it features a Vortech supercharger, Doug Thorley headers, Bowler transmission upgrades, Corsa exhaust, SSBC brakes, Eibach sway bars, and Air Lift suspension. *Photo courtesy of Trent's Trick Upholstery*

22 The Pratt & Miller C6RS was inspired by the company's Le Mans–winning Corvette C6.R race cars, but it offers daily drivability. The purpose-built carbon fiber body enhances aerodynamics. It's also 1.6 inches wider than stock, with an 8.2-liter Katech Performance small-block, computer-controlled suspension, BBS wheels, and Brembo Gran Turismo brakes. George Bunting owns this 2009, which is serial #006. *Photo courtesy of Pratt & Miller*

23 The 2010 Roush 540RH Mustang stands out for its subtlety. This 540-horsepower sleeper is capable of running 11.8-second ETs at 121 miles per hour. It uses the engine that debuted in the 2009 Roush P-51B Mustang: a 4.6-liter, three-valve mill rebuilt by Roush with forged aluminum pistons, forged steel rods and crank, and an R2300 Roush supercharger. *Photo courtesy of Roush Performance*

20

21

22
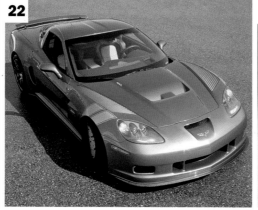

23

24 YearOne offers the limited-production, hand-built '77 Burt Reynolds Edition Trans Am in different performance levels. The top performer, *Bandit III*, comes with billet Snowflake wheels, a five-speed manual and a choice of three engines. Other updates include projector headlights, LED taillights, integrated driving lights and brake ducts, flush-mount glass, and mini-tubs. *Photo courtesy of YearOne, all rights reserved*

25 Lingenfelter is offering a 750-horsepower supercharged engine and performance package for the 2010 Camaro SS. The 7.0-liter LS7 features a Magnuson/Eaton TVS2300 supercharger, forged JE pistons, Corsa stainless exhaust, and Lingenfelter six-bolt LS9 twin-disk flywheel and clutch assembly. In the handling department, it gets Lingenfelter double-adjustable Sachs shocks, heavy-duty Driveshaft Shop halfshafts, Brembo brakes, and Hotchkis springs, sway bars, and subframe brace.

The Strikers

Hulst Customs believes diesels are the next street machine frontier. The company's first turnkey Ford Super Duty was the 2007 *Striker* (right), a turbodiesel dualie F-350 with styling inspired by the original Shelby Cobra, including the hood, front fascia, and inset grille. It sports a Banks Power Big Hoss Bundle, good for a gain of up to 138 horsepower and 231 lb-ft of torque. Other dramatic mods include the 4.5-inch side pipes, DJM suspension, mini-tubs, 24-inch American Force forged wheels wrapped in low-profile Pirelli tires, side vents, cab lights, Katzkin leather, and a Sony Xplod sound system—enough to win this truck a Ford Design Excellence Award at the SEMA Show.

Hulst followed it up with the 2009 *Striker II*, inspired by the Shelby GT500KR King of the Road Mustang. This turnkey F-350's option list is huge. The black truck shown here boasts massive power thanks to Spartan Diesel Technologies performance upgrades, which crank up the boost, change the computer tuning, and swap out the exhaust and intercoolers. Both the silver and black trucks also wear a slew of Hulst pieces, including the mesh grilles, front fascias, hood scoops, side vents, and tool boxes, and the silver truck is dressed in Badass Blue Le Mans–style stripes and Katzkin snakeskin-textured leather upholstery. *Photos courtesy of Hulst Customs*

Chapter 4
Engines & Exhaust

The engine obviously is the heart of any street machine. Absent a seriously high-performance mill, all you've got is a pretty show car . . . or perhaps a mild custom. But give a car some guts—and the drivetrain and suspension to back it up—and you've got the makings of a true street machine.

Now, how you choose to make that power is entirely a matter of budget and personal preference. You can choose the Pro Street, blower-through-the-hood look or opt for a stealthier, more low-profile turbo-

charged or supercharged setup. Or perhaps you're the hardcore all-motor, no-power-adder type.

Whether you like fuel injection or carburetion—or fuel injection that looks like carburetion—there are myriad possibilities out there today. You can rebuild a vintage engine, get a new vintage-style block, or go for a late-model crate engine. You name it, it's doable. It's really just a matter of what you want to throw you back in your seat. That said, here are a host of ideas to get you thinking.

1 A 600-cubic-inch big-block powers the 1961 Ford Starliner that ProRides built for Summit Racing. The engine is based on a Ford Racing 460-inch aluminum block, with a Crower crank and rods, JE 10.4:1 forged pistons, Comp Cams solid roller, and Trick Flow A460 aluminum heads and tunnel ram. Pretty, yes, and it makes 920 horsepower and 810 lb-ft of torque, all motor. *Photo © Summit Racing Equipment*

2 *Razor*, Erv Woller's 1969 Camaro, won Goodguys' Street Machine of the Year award in 2008 (the second year in a row that a Ringbrothers-built car won). The GM Performance all-aluminum, 545-cubic-inch Ram Jet ZL1 crate engine looks particularly trick with the body-color intake, valve covers, and headers, and it's hooked to a Viper T56 transmission.

3 Trent's Trick Upholstery did some serious stylizing under the hood of this 2010 Camaro SS, which also benefits from a Vortech supercharger, Doug Thorley headers, Corsa straight-through exhaust, and automatic transmission mods by Bowler.

4 Keasler Racing built the low-profile intake and Bobby Alloway's shop used eight Viper throttle bodies from Accufab to create a one-of-a-kind, old road racing–style induction setup for Ken Nester's 1970 Challenger. The injectors and fuel rails are mounted under the intake. Hemi experts Hensley Performance built the 740-horsepower, 509-cubic-inch engine using an Indy Cylinder Head block, Callies crank, Manley H-beam rods, and Ross pistons.

5 Note how the custom sheet metal in the engine compartment of Kendall Simmons' '72 Chevelle embraces the air cleaner. Every panel was fabricated by RPM Hot Rods, including the inner fenders, radiator support, firewall, and wheelwells. The 454-cubic-inch big-block also sports fuel injection and great graphics on the body-color valve covers.
Photo © Goodguys Rod & Custom Association

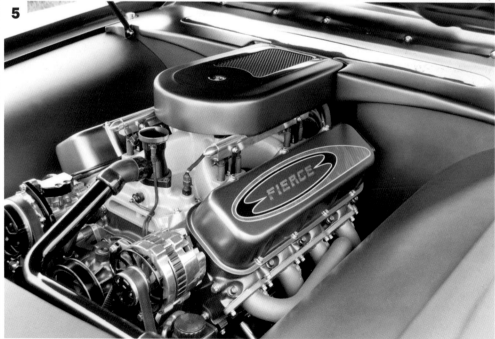

The LS1

GM's LS1 5.7-liter crate engine fits beautifully under the hood of everything from a C1 Corvette to a C-10 pickup.

The LS1 debuted in 1997, making it the first member of the LS family of V-8 small-blocks. They're radically different in design from earlier Chevy/GM small-blocks, thanks in part to a deep-skirt, six-bolt-main block with a structural oil pan.

The engine comes from GM rated at 350 horsepower and 365 lb-ft of torque, and it includes a GTO-style oil pan, electronic drive-by-wire throttle body, intake manifold, exhaust manifolds, fuel rail with injectors, balancer, and 14-inch automatic transmission flexplate. Companies like Street & Performance offer everything else you'll need to make one of these engines work in a particular application, from wiring harnesses to oil pans.

Shown here: Bryan Frank's '69 Trans Am (top left), which won Goodguys' 2009 Muscle Machine of the Year; Ryan Brockbank's '61 Corvette with its Lingenfelter-supercharged, 600-horsepower LS1 (top right); Gary Calkins' 1957 Chevy Bel Air (lower left); and Marquez Design's 1969 Chevy C-10 pickup, which used a Street & Performance wiring harness and Early Classic Enterprises LS1 motor mounts. The Hedman kit shown here makes it easy to install an LS engine in a 1978 to 1987 G-body, including Buick Regals and Grand Nationals.

Photo © Goodguys Rod & Custom Association

Photo courtesy of Marquez Design

Photo courtesy of Hedman Hedders

6 Spectre Performance's '71 Z28 still runs the original LT1. It was rebuilt recently with Air Flow Research heads, an Edelbrock Air Gap intake, a roller cam, and programmable fuel injection using an AccuFab throttle body. The valve covers are Spectre ProFab aluminum with—the show-stopping feature—a dual cold air intake setup called SpeedBySpectre ProFab Muscle Car TrakPak. *Photo courtesy of Spectre Performance*

7 Where's the supercharger? Tucked under the intake runners, of course. This 1970 Dodge Challenger convertible was rescued from New Orleans after Hurricane Katrina. Delaney Auto Design built it using a Mopar Performance 392 Hemi crate engine with a Saleen supercharger package.

8 Jay Leno's 1966 Olds Toronado project turned into something of a development mule for GM Performance Parts. The one-off, prototype 425-cubic-inch small-block uses a modified aluminum block and cylinder heads from the Cadillac CTS-V racing program. Leno's twin-turbo, intercooled beast produces 1,070 horsepower at 6,350 rpm and 1,000 lb-ft of torque at 4,750 rpm. *Photo courtesy of General Motors*

9 Steve and Lisa Caspary built their '55 Chevy, which sports a 575-horsepower, 400-cubic-inch small-block with Holley Stealth Ram fuel injection and Brodix heads linked to a Turbo 400. Renteria Brothers Custom Shop handled the metal fabrication and paint, including crafting a new core support/cover to embrace the radiator.

6

7

8

9

Mix & Match

Want to be different? Anybody can put a Chevy engine in a Ford. These folks went a whole 'nother route. Clockwise from top left: Dwayne Richardson tapped Hot Rods & Custom Stuff to build and install a 1957-vintage Dodge Hemi engine that now displaces 355 cubic inches in his '53 Ford F-100. Bill Harrison opted for a blown LS1 mated to a six-speed for his '59 International pickup. Jeff Mulvihill got really crazy—and achieved better weight balance—by shifting the 514-cubic-inch Ford all the way back into the engine compartment of his '56 Chevy. Little Joe's Street Rod Shop stuck a 1,350-horsepower blown 572 Hemi, plumbed for nitrous, both under and through the hood of this 1970 Silver Shadow, aka the world's fastest Rolls-Royce. And Erik and Paul Hansen had Strange Motion Rod & Custom install a 500-cubic-inch Cadillac engine topped with six chromed Demon two-barrel carbs in their '52 Buick.

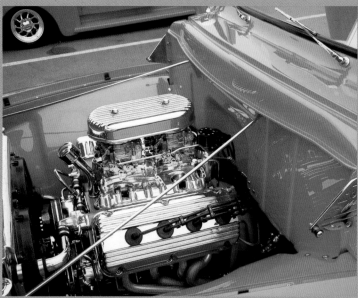

10 Shakers have always looked cool, and Classic Design Concepts offers new shaker cold air intake systems for late-model Challengers, Chargers, F-150s, and Mustangs. This Challenger system for the 6.1-liter Hemi routes air through the factory airbox, which gets retrofitted with a high-flow cone air filter. The scoop is stamped steel, and the engine cover is molded PC-ABS plastic. *Photo courtesy of CDC*

11 In creating this concept for a new Hemi 'Cuda convertible, Mr. Norm's Garage swapped the stock internals in a Gen III Hemi for a much stronger forged crank, rods, and pistons and increased the displacement to 7 liters (aka 426 cubic inches). A Kenne Bell 2.8-liter twin-screw supercharger boosts horsepower to 725. *Photo courtesy of Performance West Group*

12 The 650-horsepower LS2 in RideTech's *Velocity* Camaro breathes through a set of newly developed 2-inch tube headers from Dynatech. Fuel, ignition, and transmission electronics for the '68 Camaro are controlled by a BigStuff3 EFI system and MSD electronic ignition. The transmission is a ZF six-speed built by Bowler. *Photo courtesy of RideTech*

13 Tony and Debra Russotti's '55 Bel Air sports a cool custom air cleaner housing, which uses four K&N clamp-on flange filters.

14 Turn Key Engine Supply built the LS7 that powers Barry Blomquist's '62 Corvette, producing 618 horsepower and 640 lb-ft of torque. The carbon fiber rocker covers match the intake tubes on the Kinsler crossram, while a FAST XFI controls the tune. The 2-inch primary headers are custom stainless pieces, as is the entire aluminum engine compartment. *Photo © Goodguys Rod & Custom Association*

15 There's nothing subtle about the 1967 *Obsidian SG-One* Mustang. With twin Rotrex superchargers, twin Spearco intercoolers, a Hogan custom aluminum intake manifold, and AccuFab twin throttle bodies, the 392-cubic-inch Windsor-based engine produces 847.8 horsepower and 770 lb-ft of torque on California 91-octane fuel. That's good for 0-to-60 in less than 3 seconds. *Photo by Nick Nacca, courtesy of ScoCar*

16 Foose Design applied California Gold to the block and intake on the Mopar 392 Hemi crate engine in the *Terracuda*; the color matches the stripe scheme on this '70 Plymouth Barracuda. The custom-painted valve covers wear the same period-correct, cartoon-style fish that Chip Foose created to grace the car's quarter panels.

17 Neat, shiny, and low-profile: The EFI Merlin 540-cubic-inch big-block in Greg and Terri Merrell's '67 Chevelle sports a Hogan intake manifold, Edelbrock Performer RPM heads, an MSD distributor, a Zoops front drive assembly, and a BigStuff3 engine management system. Performance Associates built the car. Note the tight fit for the custom headers, which flow into a custom 3-inch, mandrel-bent exhaust system with an X-pipe.

Braces

Vehicles that make a whole lot of power often need extra support under the hood so they avoid torquing the body. Strut tower braces, down bars that are part of a roll cage, and other underhood strengthening devices can make a huge difference—and they can be played up or de-emphasized, depending on your taste. Clockwise from top left: Nathan Powell's '69 Camaro, Steve Broscoe's Pro Touring '69 Camaro, the '64 Fairlane called *Afterburner* built by Ringbrothers for Kenneth Smith of S&S Cycle, the Pro Touring '70 Chevelle built by RS Performance Concepts, and East Bay Muscle Cars' NOS Fogger-equipped '70 Mustang fastback.

Photo © Goodguys Rod & Custom Association

Photo courtesy of Mothers

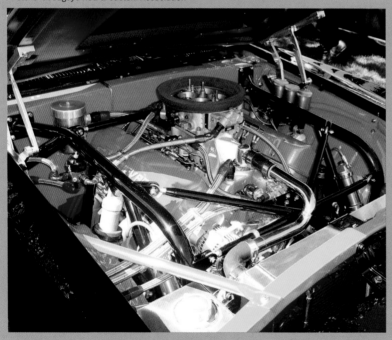

18

19

20

21

18 Fesler Built did a phenomenal job of modernizing the engine compartment of its 1970 Nova SS project car. The body-color paint underhood helps create a clean look. The GM Performance LS7 crate engine boasts a Vintage Air FrontRunner system and air conditioning, with a Magnaflow SS custom exhaust. Also note the Fesler billet hood hinges. *Photo courtesy of Fesler Built*

19 Darren Tedder won the 2008 DynoMax Power to the Wheels challenge in the nonpower-adder class with his tunnel ram–equipped 654-cubic-inch Hemi. The '71 Cuda managed to send an amazing 956.83 horsepower to the rear wheels without the use of nitrous, turbos, or superchargers. *Photo courtesy of DynoMax*

20 The '68 Wraith Mustang is powered by a Shelby 427 aluminum FE block that's been bored and stroked to 482 cubic inches. It's topped with an aluminum sheetmetal tunnel ram–style manifold, aluminum heads, a fuel injection system with 150-pound injectors, and a ProCharger F1-R centrifugal blower with an air-to-air intercooler, good for 900 horsepower at the flywheel on pump gas. *Photo courtesy of Wraith Motorsports*

21 The carbs on Tom Heaton's blown '65 Corvette are a great example of the kind of work done by Holley's Custom Shop. If you want to personalize anything from carburetors and intake manifolds to blower cases and water pumps, the shop will do custom polishing and chrome, black chrome, and 24K gold plating, plus powder-coating in 29 different colors. It's a useful, if little-known, service.

Photo courtesy of Ford

Engine Covers

One way to make an engine compartment look spectacular is with a custom engine cover. From left: Michael's Rod Shop built the stunning cover with twin breathers (and the custom valve covers) for the 454-cubic-inch big-block Chevy in Harold Robinson's 1956 F-100. Ford's Living Legends Design Studio and the Ford Performance Group created a beautiful underhood appearance for the Supercharged Thunderbird concept car; nice touches include the vintage-style V-8 emblem and Thunderbird script on the carbon fiber coil covers. The 572-cubic-inch big-block in Phil Ray's 1957 Bel Air convertible sports a color-matched engine cover that works with a dual cold air intake system.

22 It may seem as if all Mopars have a Hemi these days, but Purpose Built's 1969 515 GTB Dodge Charger has a Mopar Performance all-aluminum 515 Wedge under the hood. Pure Vision Design built the car to have a late '60s Ferrari/European road race car feel. Ray Barton Racing Engines built the engine and Passon Performance the aluminum A833 18-spline overdrive four-speed transmission.

23

23 Classic Recreations' version of the iconic *Eleanor* Mustang comes with a custom-built 410-cubic-inch Keith Craft Racing 351W stroker motor with forged internals and, if you so choose, a supercharger or nitrous. You also get a Concept One serpentine drive belt system, braided stainless fuel lines, and air conditioning, with either a Tremec TKO manual or a four-speed automatic transmission. *Photo courtesy of Classic Recreations*

24

24 Surprise! A Viper 8.4-liter all-aluminum V-10 actually will fit under the hood of a new Dodge Challenger. Of course, Chrysler SRT Engineering may have spent more time and money than most humans can afford, but the 2009 Dodge Challenger SRT10 Concept now womps out an impressive 600 horsepower and 560 lb-ft of torque—and it just plain looks cool.

25

25 Nelson Racing Engines' Supercar #003 is a 1984 Camaro with 1,750 horsepower at 5,800 rpm and 1,680 lb-ft of torque at 4,900 rpm—yet it idles at 800 rpm. It features NRE's 427 Twin Turbo Hot Rod Series crate engine with a patented NRE billet intake, dual injector intake manifold with fuel regulation, and patented NRE turbos.

26 Bryce Customs designed this '68 Dodge Dart and Ray Barton Engineering built it. The Mopar Performance 572-cubic-inch crate Hemi now produces 850 horsepower and 750 lb-ft of torque, good enough for wheel-standing performance, 9-second quarter-miles, and 0-to-60 in the 2-second range. It's mated to Rockland Standard Gear's Tranzilla six-speed manual gearbox, built to handle up to 1,200 horsepower and 1,000 lb-ft of torque.

Photo courtesy of Jeffrey's Custom Conversions

NASCAR Themes

In case you haven't noticed, NASCAR racing is kind of popular. So it's no surprise that some people choose a NASCAR theme for their street machines.

Top: Jeffrey's Custom Conversions' Super Street Series Stock Cars come with a Chevrolet ZZ4 350-cubic-inch, 355-horsepower NASCAR engine—with a two-year, 24,000-mile warranty, no less. The rest of the drivetrain includes a four-speed transmission with Hurst shifter, a racing bellhousing, a high-performance hydraulic clutch, a Stock Car driveshaft and yokes, and a 9-inch Ford full floater rear differential with a locker.

Bottom: YearOne teamed up with Gillette Evernham Racing, Musclecar TV, and celebrity Bill Goldberg to update a legend, the NASCAR Superbird. This 1970 Plymouth now sports a current NASCAR-spec 358-cubic-inch Dodge engine. In nonrestrictor trim, but detuned enough to run on pump gas, it produces 800 horsepower. In other words, it makes 2.24 horsepower *per cubic inch*. The motor's backed up by a super-light Tex Racing four-speed manual and an 8 3/4 rear.

Weber-Style Carbs & EFI

Weber carburetors just plain look cool, but vintage Webers are getting pretty hard to find and, therefore, pricey. Plus, plenty of folks prefer fuel injection to carburetion these days. So several companies have come up with Weber-style looks that offer engine builders options, and Weber North America has also begun reissuing carburetors.

Among the choices: Inglese (top left) has created its own Weber-esque 48 IDA two-barrel carburetors (as with original Webers, the "48" means 48mm bore diameter and throttle plate, and "IDA" indicates this is a high-performance downdraft carburetor), shown here on a '67 Camaro with a 383/425-horsepower GM crate engine.

Dynatek Racing created the Dynatek Classic Fuel Injection (CFI) system (top right) that looks like Weber 48 housings but is actually a complete individual-runner EFI system able to flow up to 2,300 cfm. It's shown here on the 485-horsepower, 347-cubic-inch Boss 347 engine in Classic Design Concepts' *Bullitt Flashback* Mustang.

Bob Ream at Imagine Injection also came up with a Weber-style—as well as a Hilborn-style—EFI system, like the ones shown here on the World Products–built 572-cubic-inch all-aluminum Hemi in Modern Muscle's 1971 Pro Touring Cuda (bottom left) and the Gen III 6.1-liter Hemi in the '71 Challenger R/T resto-mod built by Mr. Norm's Garage (second row).

PFC Enterprises' ITB intake features eight 58mm throttle bodies with a central vacuum accumulator, and the aluminum fuel rails feed SRT-4 Stage II injectors, as shown here on Plum Floored Creations' *Mutant Bee* (third row), which sports a 598-horsepower 6.1 Hemi.

And TWM Induction (bottom right) makes the throttle-body fuel injection system—complete with inlet manifold, fuel rails, and fuel pressure regulator—used on the 6.1 Hemi in Brett Hunter's '70 Cuda.

Photo courtesy of CDC

Photo courtesy of Performance West Group

Photo courtesy of Plum Floored Creations

Photo courtesy of Performance West Group

Photo © Goodguys Rod & Custom Association

27 Got a big blower with a scoop sticking through the hood? It may block your view forward, but it's a convenient place to mount a rearview mirror, as Terry Henry did on his '48 Oldsmobile.

28 Doug Schultz built his '66 Fairlane, including the beautifully formed engine compartment that's now home to a Ford Motorsport 635-horsepower, 514-cubic-inch big-block. He even built his own multiport sequential fuel injection setup. Impressive.

29 Steve's Auto Restoration built this '57 Ford F-100, which has a gorgeous engine installation. That's a '96 Mustang Cobra 4.6-liter DOHC engine with a Kenne Bell TS1000-96C twin-screw supercharger that produces 15 pounds of boost. Perfect symmetry is achieved with those 3-inch polished stainless air intake tubes. It exhales via JBA 2.5-inch long-tube headers and Flowmaster Hush Power II mufflers.

30 Yep, it really is a diesel. Mike Racke built the 6.6-liter Duramax V-8 for his '70 Chevelle. By upgrading the turbos (now making 30 psi of boost), installing Carrillo steel rods, swapping in a bigger solid-roller cam, and CNC porting the factory heads, he more than tripled the engine's power figures—up to 950 horsepower and 1,700 lb-ft of torque, while getting 32 miles per gallon.

31 Not one, but two Supercharger USA 6-71 blowers with shotgun-style scoops sit side by side atop a custom intake manifold on the 355-cubic-inch small-block in Ron and Rosie Smith's '56 Chevy pickup, aptly named *Insane*. Ron and Rosie are the RSs in RS & RS Speed Shop. (Don Hampton offers intake manifolds that will make this sort of twin Roots-style supercharger setup possible, if you're tempted.)

32

33

34

35

36

32 Ron's Motorworks built Glen Baugus' stunning '72 Barracuda, with a Gen III 6.1-liter Hemi under the hood. A pair of Paxton Novi 1200 superchargers boost output to almost 700 horsepower.

33 We've seen some tight engine compartments. Now check out how much room there is under the hood of a '72 Chevy Monte Carlo (in this case, Robert Cardena's small-block car). With the engine set way back, the Monte—and its GM cousin, the Pontiac Grand Prix—offered impressive handling. Great starting point for a street machine . . . I'm just sayin'.

34 For Bruce Pettingill's '64 Chevelle, Hot Rods & Customs built custom plates that close up the A-arm cutouts in the wheelwells. They hid the Kugel dual aluminum brake master cylinder, hid the hoses and hardware, and camouflaged the Kugel dual reservoir filler on the firewall. Plus, they built custom panels in the front corners of the fenders to hide wiring and air conditioning hoses.

35 Forced-induction expert Kenny Duttweiler built the 525-cubic-inch, all-aluminum Ford big-block with a Paxton Novi 2000 Super charger for Summit Racing's '95 Mustang GT called *QuikStang*. On the dyno at 15 psi, the engine made 958 horsepower and 863 lb-ft of torque. Kenny says if you add another 5 pounds of boost, you're looking at 1,000 horsepower. *Photo © Summit Racing Equipment*

36 The song-inspiring 409 engine in Dick Long's '63 Impala was stroked using a 454 crank, creating 482 cubic inches. With two four-barrel carbs, a solid-lifter roller, and tubular headers, it produced 500 horsepower and more than 500 lb-ft of torque. Car builder Barry Gates also smoothed the firewall and ditched the stock heater, installing a smaller, more efficient under-dash unit.

37 The shaved engine bay in the prototype Jim Wangers Signature Edition GTO from Big 3 Performance is home to a Butler Performance–built 505-cubic-inch fuel-injected Pontiac V-8. The IA2 cast-iron block is topped with FAST EFI and CNC-ported Edelbrock aluminum heads. Custom headers flow into dual exhaust, and the Viper-spec TR6060 six-speed sends power to a 3.73-geared Ford 9-inch. *Photo courtesy of Jim Wangers*

Same Concept, Very Different Execution

Left: Deane Palmer's Shelby CS8 from Hillbank Motor Sports started off as a regular Mustang GT. Now it makes 416 rear-wheel horsepower and runs 12.24 at 111 miles per hour in the quarter-mile, thanks in large part to an intercooled Shelby Performance Parts/Paxton Novi supercharger setup that produces 12 pounds of boost, plus a 2.5-inch Magnaflow dual exhaust with X-pipe.

Right: Drake Muscle Cars' 2006 Mustang also boasts a Shelby Performance Parts/Paxton supercharger system and oodles of Shelby Performance Parts, but it couldn't look more different under the hood.

38

38 The engine compartment in Mike Jordan's '62 Chevy II achieves a perfect balance of black and yellow and shiny. The BDS blower on this 428 is topped off with BDS's 16-nozzle EFI plate assembly, which comes with 42-pound injectors and that incredibly beautiful hard-line plumbing.

39 The black and copper styling theme on Kevin and Karen Alstott's '68 Camaro is most noticeable under the hood. Lakeside Rods and Rides built the custom engine surround and transformed a '35 Ford headlight bucket into a voluptuous cover for the master cylinder. The 355-cubic-inch small-block exhales through Sanderson headers and Flowmaster Super 44 3-inch exhaust. *Photo courtesy of Lakeside Rods*

40 A whole lot of smooth metal and red paint are set off by the shiny intake manifold and valve covers. Roger Woody once said the engine compartment in his '55 Chevy pickup was so big it needed a big engine. So he opted for a GM 8100 Vortec, which displaces 8.1 liters or 496 cubic inches. It was built by Street & Performance.

41 Steve Schalk did most of the work on his '66 Chevy II Nova. The 572-inch aluminum big-block features an induction system that Steve helped design, which works with an intake manifold from Morrison Motorsports of Australia. The engine also boasts an ACCEL DFI engine management system and AmFor Electronics alternator and charging system.

Other Crate Engine Options

You've seen a fair number of crate engine installations in this chapter, since crate engines can be more affordable than custom-built—and even home-built—mills. Here are a few more options from engine-building experts with serious racing credentials.

Clockwise from top left: Roush Performance offers Ford-based crate engines that range in size from 327 to 588 cubic inches, like this 588RX. You can choose electronic fuel injection or single- or multicarb setups, with power outputs ranging up to 630 horses and 690 lb-ft of torque.

Jon Kaase Racing Engines' new Boss Nine crate engine is a modern-day Ford Boss 429. The new high-nodular cast-iron block can accommodate 429, 460, 521, and 600-cubic-inch buildups, producing from 500 to 1,000 streetable horsepower.

Banks Power offers a 6.0-liter twin-turbo small-block Chevy that's race shop–assembled and dyno tested. It features a Banks/Dart high-nickel iron block, Banks blower pistons, and exclusive Banks/Dart aluminum cylinder heads. The ACCEL/DFI engine management system is factory-tuned to the buyer's power and fuel octane requirements, with calibrations for up to 1,000 horsepower.

And World Products has collaborated with 409 tuning wizard Lamar Walden to create a brand-new aluminum Chevrolet 409 block that's 140 pounds lighter than the original factory block. It also incorporates about 25 technical innovations. The new design features four-bolt mains instead of two, the main bearing journals have been redesigned to accept today's superior high-performance bearings, and the cylinder bores are now 4.5 inches instead of 4.3125, so the engine can breathe better and rev faster and higher. World is manufacturing the block, and Walden is offering complete engines.

Photo courtesy of Roush Performance

Photo courtesy of Jon Kaase

Photo courtesy of World Products

Photo courtesy of Banks Power

42 Modern Muscle's '69 Mustang sports a Ford Racing 5.4-liter V-8 with a Kenne Bell twin-screw supercharger and intercooler and a FAST engine management system. To make it fit, they moved the firewall back, removed the shock towers, installed a Heidt's Mustang II–style front suspension and crossmember, and moved the master cylinder under the dash. *Photo courtesy of Performance West Group*

43 Tom Boldry likes to race in SCCA GTA events, so his '69 Charger, built by Rock's Rod & Custom, features a 472-cubic-inch Hemi with Indy aluminum cylinder heads and Mass-Flow fuel injection. Boldry shifts the Tremec TKO 650 five-speed using a custom pistol grip shifter with an integrated line lock. *Photo © Goodguys Rod & Custom Association*

44 Steve's Restorations & Hot Rods built its '56 Ford F-100 to be an environmentally friendly hot rod. The 460-cubic-inch Ford big-block sports aluminum heads, a tunnel ram intake, and numerous performance mods, but what really sets it apart is the fuel: It runs on liquid propane. Steve's also fabbed the stunning copper engine compartment.

45 Forget about the way billet looked in the 1980s. Check out the hot Imagine Injection setup on this 351 Cleveland. The engine originally lived in a Pantera. It now resides under the hood of a '51 Ford convertible, giving the car its name: *Pantera's Box.*

46 Check out the 5-inch engine setback in Modern Muscle's '69 Camaro, which rides on an Art Morrison MaxG chassis. The cowl has been notched to accommodate the air cleaners. The Dart 565 cast-iron big-block with Hilborn FI by Imagine Injection sends 650 horsepower through a Pro Motion TKO 600 transmission and a C5 Corvette Z06 differential with Rockland Standard 4.10 gears. *Photo courtesy of Performance West Group*

GM's New E-Rod Package

GM Performance Parts' new E-Rod crate engine package, shown here in GM's '55 Chevy E-Rod, includes the same basic LS3 engine that's found in the Camaro SS and Corvette (additional engine choices, including the LS7 and LSA, are planned for future packages). The 6.2-liter crate engine is rated at 430 horsepower and 424 lb-ft of torque. GMPP worked closely with CARB and SEMA officials to develop the CARB-approved system, which also includes a GMPP LS3 engine wiring harness and engine control module, exhaust manifolds, catalytic converters, oxygen sensors and sensor bosses, a fuel tank evaporative emissions canister, a mass airflow sensor and sensor boss, an accelerator pedal (for use with the LS3's electronic throttle), and an air filter.

Photo courtesy of General Motors

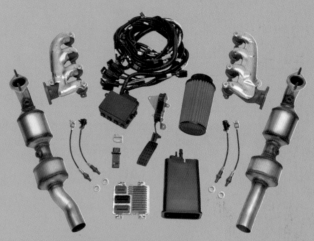

Photo courtesy of General Motors

47 Drag racing legend Bill "Grumpy" Jenkins and Smeding Performance built the 572-cubic-inch big-block in Dave and Karen Leisinger's '67 Camaro, and Jenkins autographed the valve cover. The Lakeside Rods–built car also sports a PRC radiator, Lemons headers, 4L85E transmission, and a trick engine cover with graphics to match the body. *Photo courtesy of Lakeside Rods*

47

48

49

50

48 The shaker scoop atop Devan Glissmeyer's 418-cubic-inch Ford may not be functional, but the ATI ProCharger certainly is. Check the slick routing to and from the intercooler, which gets played up beautifully by the custom metalwork in this Kindig-it Design–built '68 Mustang. *Photo © Goodguys Rod & Custom Association*

49 *Voila!* The most anticipated new engine by street machine enthusiasts, the supercharged LS9 that made its debut in the 2009 Corvette ZR1, has been impressively installed under the hood of Dan Ferrara's 2010 Camaro SS. Street & Performance handled the install using S&P headers feeding into a Magnaflow 3-inch exhaust. In this configuration, the engine is making 635 horsepower and 604 lb-ft of torque.

50 Josiah Coy built his '65 GTO convertible with a 455-cubic-inch, Tri-Power Pontiac that makes 504 horsepower and 539 lb-ft of torque. It sends power through a five-speed and 3.73:1 gears, and Josiah figures it will run 11.3 in the quarter. The car rides on a Schwartz Performance prototype frame, and it won a GM Design Award for Best Midsize Vehicle at the 2009 SEMA Show.

51 Ed Martinez, president of PSE Superchargers, added twin Lysholm 1600AX blowers to the 5.4-liter engine in his 2004 Ford SVT Lightning pickup. He also upgraded to set of ported 2006 Ford GT four-valve heads, Manley rods, CP custom pistons, a forged crank, 78-pound injectors and, of course, a totally custom intake setup. The result: 960 horsepower.

52 Grand Touring Garage built the 600-horsepower '65 Ford 427 single overhead camshaft engine that powers the '70 Mustang called *Trans-Cammer*. The custom cowl induction–style aluminum air cleaner picks up fresh air from the windshield area. GTG also fabricated the water overflow tank, mounted the power steering reservoir in front of the driver's side cylinder head, and mounted the alternator facing the engine. *Photo courtesy of Grand Touring Garage*

53 To make sure the 540-cubic-inch, 600-horsepower big-block in their 1969 Phase III Camaro could exhale properly, the folks at Baldwin-Motion installed a set of full-length Hooker headers, which feed into a mandrel-bent, 3-inch dual exhaust system. This setup includes an X-pipe to increase power and fuel economy. *Photo courtesy of Baldwin-Motion*

54 There's a reason sculptor/car guy Mike Cooper has become renowned for his headers. Check out the ones he built for his own ride, a crazy '33 Ford pickup called the *Tubester*. The twisted tubes are hooked to a 355-cubic-inch Chevy small-block with a 6-71 Littlefield blower, and they empty through a collector muffler.

55 The folks at Modern Muscle modified the Art Morrison MaxG chassis under their '69 Camaro Supercar to route and mount the dual exhaust system. It also received a pair of Flowmaster mufflers. *Photo courtesy of Performance West Group*

69

56 Dutchman's '57 Bel Air features beautiful billet signature exhaust hangers. You can also sneak a peek at the independent rear suspension and custom-fabricated polished exhaust system made with Magnaflow mandrel-bent tubing. *Photo courtesy of RenovatioLucis.com*

57 If you've made a lot of engine mods to your first-gen Camaro and it just isn't performing up to your expectations, this could be why: The double-wall factory exhaust tubing may look just fine on the outside, but it can become extremely restrictive on the inside. This damage wasn't caused by impact, but rather by heat and time. *Photo courtesy of Flowmaster*

58 The exhaust system on this 720-horsepower '69 Camaro was configured with traditional-style cutouts, so it can go from street-legal to uncorked and race-ready in no time. *Photo courtesy of CARS Inc.*

59 Bill Sherman races this street/strip '63 Falcon, which sports an EFI Windsor with dramatic twin turbochargers, K&N air filters, a Holley throttle body and an MSD HVC II coil. *Photo courtesy of Max Nealon*

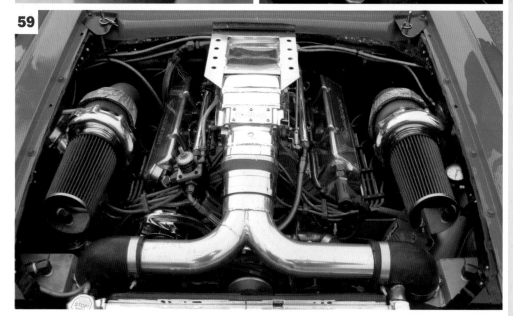

Exhaust Exits

Photo courtesy of HPP

Photo courtesy of Cherry Bomb

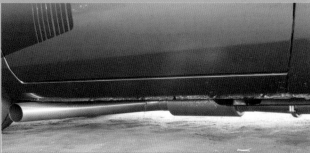

Photo courtesy of DynoMax

Photo courtesy of CDC

Photo courtesy of Steve's Restorations

1

Chapter 5
Wheels & Tires

Wheels and tires make a huge difference in the way a vehicle looks—perhaps more than any other styling choice.

And the combinations are nearly limitless. These days, street machines are riding on wheels that range from 15 to 24 inches in diameter, in finishes ranging from polished to matte, and from black to body color.

Of course, wheels and tires also dramatically affect a vehicle's performance—and not just in terms of their ability to accelerate and corner. Wheels and tires are unsprung weight, and increasing this weight dramatically affects a vehicle's acceleration and stopping abilities—another factor to consider when wheel shopping.

As for tires, at one time, the really wide rear rubber was reserved for Pro Streeters and serious street/strip machines, but now g-machines are running wide back tires and kicking butt in autocrosses.

The wheel and tire setups here are sure to get you thinking. I've even grouped some of the photos by vehicle make and model so you can fully appreciate how much of a styling difference rolling stock makes.

2 Boyd Coddington Crown Jewel wheels really set off the Sherwin-Williams B-5 Super Blue paint on this '71 Plymouth GTX resto-mod, with its Van Gordon Racing–built 440+6. The wheels are 18x7s up front, 18x8s rear, with Pirelli PZero Rosso 245/45ZR15 and 255/55ZR18 tires. *Photo courtesy of Performance West Group*

3 The five-spoke center design creates a sort of alternating-spoke effect for these one-off billet wheels on Kirk Johnson's 1968 F-100. They were made by EVOD Industries, and they're 18 inches front, 20 rear, with BFGoodrich g-Force tires. *Photo © Goodguys Rod & Custom Association*

4 Once people saw the Katech ClubSport Z06 Corvette, they wanted the lightweight wheels, so Katech now offers them in a variety of colors. The single-piece 18x9.5-inch front wheels weigh just 24.5 pounds, the 19x12 rears just 26 pounds. The forged and shot peened aluminum wheels actually exceed factory standards for cornering strength by 37 percent. *Photo courtesy of Katech Performance*

Two Pairs of Shoes

Plum Floored Creations' 1970 Coronet, called *Plum Floored*, models two sets of wheels. At top, it's wearing Center Line's 18x8 and 20x9.5 Lexi two-piece forged alloy wheels with Yokohama 225/40-18 and 285/30-20 YR-rated radials. And at bottom, it's wearing the same size wheels and the exact same tires, but my how different it looks in Center Line Lazer II's. *Photos courtesy of Plum Floored Creations*

The Foose Fishtail

Chip Foose spent months perfecting the design of this wheel—not specifically for the *Terracuda*, but once that car began taking shape, it was clear this was the right rim for the project.

When that car debuted, the Foose Design wheel was a one-off, but it has since gone into production as a two-piece aluminum model called Fishtail, which comes with a polished finish.

The *Terracuda* (top) wears 19- and 20-inch Fishtails that were painted BASF California Gold to match the stripes on Darren Metropolis' '70 Barracuda.

The polished production wheel looks remarkably different—but equally attractive—on Rafael Navarro IV's 1970 454 SS El Camino. It's shod in 19x8- and 20x10-inch versions with 245/35ZR19 and 295/35ZR20 Pirelli PZeros.

Photo by Ryan Hagel, courtesy of Pirelli

Photo courtesy of Pirelli

5 The Detroit Speed & Engineering 1970 Camaro test car shows off its massive BFGoodrich T/A KDW tires during the Vendor Autocross Challenge at a Goodguys' event in Kansas in 2009. A set of Detroit Speed Deep Tubs made room for those 335s out back. *Photo courtesy of BFGoodrich*

6 Hulst Customs designed one-off wheels for Don and Karen Blacksmith's '56 Bel Air convertible. The 19x8- and 20x10-inchers are called 1320, and Hulst will begin offering them as production pieces soon.

7 Cherry Bomb's 1964 Dodge D-100 Short Bed Stepside truck is a genuine barn find, now updated with a Mopar 526 Hemi crate motor and a ladder bar rear suspension. The truck rides on vintage Radir drag slicks with wide whites in the rear and Coker Tires in the front. *Photo courtesy of Cherry Bomb*

8 There's something particularly wicked-looking—even barbaric—about a two-spoke wheel design, which is particularly fitting for Galpin Auto Sports' *Scythe,* an insanely, outrageously customized 2008 Ford Mustang GT Convertible that sports 22-inch wheels up front and 24s in the back wrapped in Pirelli Scorpion Zero tires.

9 Heide Performance Products designed the wheels for its new Challenger Daytona. They're 20x8.5 and 20x10 forged aluminum, available in a satin (shown) or polished finish. The redline tires are also an HPP exclusive based on a set of 245/35-20 and 265/35-20 Nitto 555s. *Photo courtesy of HPP*

10 Street Concepts fitted its '71 Challenger coupe with 20x8.5 and 20x11.5 GFG Trento-7 wheels. They feature a brushed face and a chrome lip, and they're dressed in Toyo S/T 245/35R20 and 305/40R20 tires. *Photo courtesy of Street Concepts*

11

11 The Roadster Shop and artist Eric Brockmeyer designed Barry Blomquist's '62 Corvette, right down to the one-off spindle-mount ForgeLine wheels. The three-piece wheels are 19 and 20 inches, wearing 275/30 and 335/30 Michelin Pilot Sport PS2s. *Photo © Goodguys Rod & Custom Association*

12

12 D & P Classic Chevy built this '65 Chevelle called *Bamboozled* on the TV show *Chop Cut Rebuild*. It rides on a set of one-off wheels built by Oasis Custom, a division of Oasis Luxury Alloys that specializes in building wheels to customers' specifications. You can order your own unique one-piece cast-aluminum or two-piece forged aluminum wheels, ranging from 10 to 26 inches.

13

13 The Toyo Proxes TQ drag radial not only looks cool, it's also totally streetable, so you can drive it to and from the drag strip. The asymmetric tread pattern works well on both straight axle and modern independent rear suspension cars. Oh yeah, and it's been shown to help in running fast and consistent ETs, too. *Photo courtesy of Toyo*

14 This street/strip Camaro is running the classic drag racing look. In this case, those are 15x3-inch Billet Specialties Comp 5 wheels up front and 15x10s in the rear, wrapped in Hoosier rubber. However, they're not streetable, since they're not built to withstand things like potholes and road debris. *Photo courtesy of Billet Specialties*

Fastback Mustangs

These fastback Mustangs are both running 17-inch wheels, but they look distinctly different. The *Trans-Cammer* '70 Mustang features 17-inch custom wheels. The center sections were CNC machined from billet aluminum and then powder-coated gray, while the rim hoops were hard anodized black. Grand Touring Garage chose BFGoodrich T/A KD tires because of their excellent handling characteristics and high-speed capabilities.

Scott Taylor's '68 Mustang rides on polished American Racing Shelby Cobra 427 wheels. The fronts are 17x8s with a 4.75-inch backspacing, and the rears are 17x9.5 with a 5.75-inch backspacing. They're wrapped in 245/45ZR and 285/40ZR BFGoodrich G-Force KDWS T/A tires.

Photo courtesy of Grand Touring Garage

Photo courtesy of Scott Taylor

Retro Wheels

It is possible to achieve a retro/classic look with modern-size wheels, either for a new vehicle or a vintage ride. For instance, California Pony Cars' new NXT-Generation one-piece, cast-aluminum wheels (top) look like the Styled Steel wheel that was optional on 1965 to 1967 Mustangs. However, the originals were 14 inches in diameter, and these SS Retro Wheels come in 17x8-inch sizes for 1965 to 1973 and 1994 to 2010 Mustangs, as well as 20x9- and 20x10-inch sizes for 2005 to 2010 'Stangs.

The Jim Wangers Signature Edition GTO (center) rolls on special Jim Wangers Signature Edition Rally II three-piece wheels that are built by HRE. They measure 19x10 inches up front and 20x12 in the rear—slightly larger than the original 15-inch Rally IIs that came on Pontiac's 1969 GTO Judge.

When Ken Lingenfelter of Lingenfelter Performance Engineering decided to transform a 2010 Chevy Camaro (bottom) into a 1971-style Pontiac Trans Am, it only made sense to run honeycomb wheels. But unlike the original 15-inchers, these custom honey-combs with bright brushed-aluminum details measure 20 inches in diameter, and they're fitted with Nitto 275/40ZR20 and 315/35ZR20 tires.

Photo courtesy of California Pony Cars

Photo courtesy of Jim Wangers

Photo courtesy of Lingenfelter Performance

15 The 18- and 20-inch Billet Specialties wheels on Summit Racing's '61 Starliner are one-offs, beautifully engraved with the word "Starliner." ProRides had to cut up the set of pristine (and pricy) new-old-stock rear quarter panels used on this car to lengthen the wheelwells so the beefy BFGoodrich Comp T/A tires would fit. *Photo © Summit Racing Equipment*

16 Center Line Convo Pro wheels give this Chevelle an old school street/strip look. The two-piece wheels come in a 15-inch diameter, with widths ranging from 4 to 15 inches—plus there's a 16x16 available for the rear. The center section has a satin/machine finish, while the outer is highly polished.

17 Most rear-drive vehicles wind up with a deep dish to the rear wheels. But this '58 Chevy pickup has a surprisingly deep dish to the front wheels too. This typically happens with a narrower frame/subframe—or with a stock setup and the wheels moved outboard. These are 18x7- and 18x8-inch Billet Specialties Vintec wheels with the optional spinner caps. *Photo courtesy of Billet Specialties*

15

16

17

Same Wheel, Different Car

Modern Muscle's two-piece forged wheel, called Muscle, is available in several different powder-coat finishes. It's shown here on: Modern Muscle's Pro Touring '69 Camaro in 19x8- and 20x10-inch sizes, with BFGoodrich gForce T/A 245/35ZR19 and 285/30-20 tires; Mr. Norm's '71 Challenger R/T resto-mod in 17x7- and 18x10-inch sizes, with BFGoodrich gForce T/A KDW 245/45ZR17 and 285/40ZR18 tires; Modern Muscle's '71 Cuda in 19x8- and 20x12-inch sizes with 245/35ZR19 and 335/30ZR20 Michelin PS2 tires; and Modern Muscle's '69 Mustang in 19x7- and 20x8-inch sizes with 235/35ZR19 and 255/35ZR20 BFGoodrich gForce T/A tires. *Photos courtesy of Performance West Group*

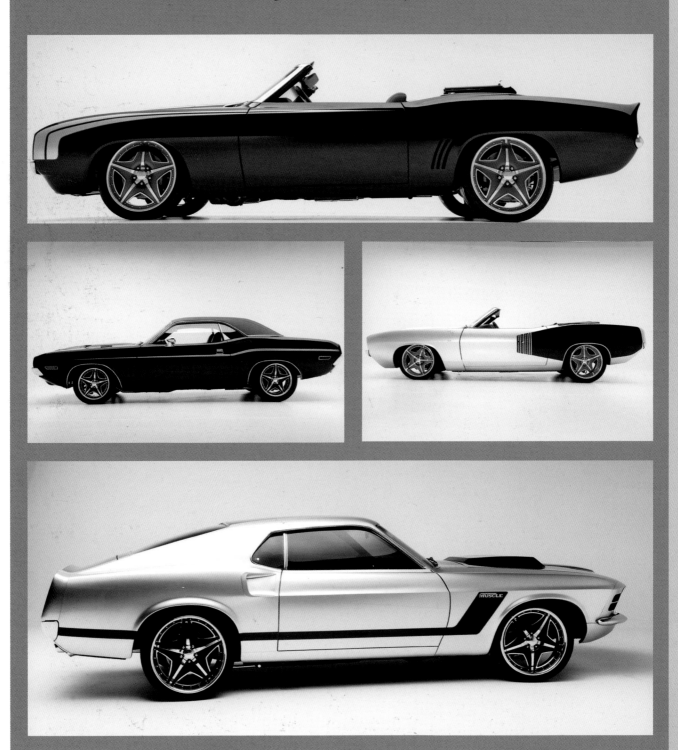

Color Matching

Color matching the wheels to a car's paint job—either the body color or an accent color—has become really popular, and there are several ways to go. You can color match the wheel face (which could be spokes, depending on the style of the wheel). You can color match any details on the face (for example, the face lines). You can add color to the side of the face or spokes (aka the window). And you can add color to the center cap, inner lip, or outer lip, as well as to the flange or flange bolts on a multi-piece wheel.

Photo courtesy of Billet Specialties

Photo courtesy of Performance West Group

Photo courtesy of The Roadster Shop

Photo by Peter Linney, courtesy of ScoCar

The New Camaro

Top left: Callaway Cars fits the limited-edition Hendrick Motorsports 25th Anniversary Camaro SS with Callaway 20x8- and 20x9-inch wheels riding on the car's original equipment tires (Pirelli P245/45ZR20 front, P275/40ZR20 rear).

The Summit White Camaro Chroma (top right) is outfitted with a full complement of Chevy accessories from GM, including the 21-inch wheels with a nice red outer lip detail.

The Fesler-Moss Camaro wears Fesler-branded 22-inch Asanti three-piece wheels.

Trent's Trick Upholstery fitted the blue-and-orange Camaro with 22-inch Bonspeed wheels with blue

hoops and Pirelli P-Zero tires, and it lowered the car a whopping 6 inches.

Forgiato's black Camaro (bottom) wears the company's Estremo wheel. The 22x9 front has a 3.5-inch lip, the 22x11 rear a 4-inch lip.

Forgiato crafted custom wide body kits for its silver and yellow Camaros to fit wider wheels under the cars. The silver Camaro wears 24x9- and 24x15-inch Forgiato Misto wheels with a 9-inch lip in the rear, wrapped in Pirelli 275/25-24 and 405/25-24 tires. The yellow car also sports 24x9- and 24x15-inchers, but they're the Forgiato Vizzo.

Photo courtesy of Callaway Cars

Photo courtesy of Fesler Built

Photo courtesy of Trent's Trick Upholstery

Photo courtesy of Forgiato

Photo courtesy of Forgiato

Photo courtesy of Forgiato

Radically Different

Want something totally different for your street machine? It's not hard to find uncommon looks, like the chrome Envy (left) and Big Ange styles from Greed Wheels. Both come with a chrome finish in 22x9.5- and 24x9.5-inch sizes. *Photos courtesy of PDK Wheels*

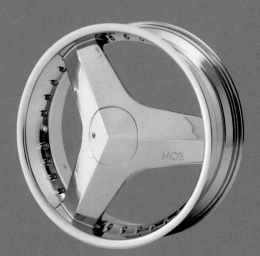

Same Basic Style, Very Different Size

Even with the same basic style of wheel, it's clear that you can achieve a very different look by changing the wheel's diameter, the tire's profile, and the vehicle's ride height.

Photo courtesy of Billet Specialties

The New Challenger

From top: The Dodge Challenger 1320 began life as a Mopar Drag Pak Challenger, a lightweight, stripped-down, race-only, special-order model designed for competitive drag racing. This street-legal version rides on 18x7.5-inch Mopar police wheels, widened to 18x9.5 in the rear and then strapped with Mickey Thompson street-legal drag radials (225/60-18s and 305/45-18s).

The red outer lip detail on the black rims beautifully matches the red pinstriping on the black-on-black Mopar Underground 2009 Challenger Blacktop. The 22-inch Dodge Viper wheels come from Factory Reproductions, and they're wrapped in 265/35R22 front and 305/30R22 Dunlop tires.

Mr. Norm's 2008 Super Challenger is shod with 20x8.5- and 20x9.5-inch Modern Muscle two-piece forged wheels, with Pirelli Scorpion Zero Assimetrico 245/45ZR20 and 265/45ZR20 tires.

George Barris and high-performance muscle car builder Steve Sanderson teamed up to create the *Red Demon*, which sports flared fenders to make room for Goodyear Eagle F1 245/45ZR20s up front and Goodyear Fortera 305/40R22s in the rear on rims that were custom made by ICCE Wheels.

Photo courtesy of Chrysler

Photo courtesy of Chrysler

Photo courtesy of Performance West Group

Chevelle Choices

Here are a few different looks for a Chevelle. At the traditional end of the spectrum, Edelbrock's '67 wears 15x7 Cragar SS wheels all around, with 225/60-15 tires up front and 255/60-15s rear.

In contrast, Hotchkis dressed this '67 Chevelle in 18x8- and 18x9.5-inch Bonspeed Clutch modular forged wheels.

The other Chevelles wear 17- and 20-inch Billet Specialties Profile Collection Rivieras (center); 20- and 22-inch Billet Specialties SLD89 wheels, otherwise known as soft-lip Vintec Dishes (bottom left); and 17-inch Intro V-Rods.

Photo courtesy of Edelbrock

Photo courtesy of Hotchkis

Photo courtesy of Billet Specialties

Photo courtesy of Billet Specialties

Back in Black

Black five-spoke wheels definitely look hot on late-model Mustangs. Summit Racing's '95 Mustang (bottom right) sports a set of American Racing Killer wheels, named after Dale Earnhardt Jr.'s boxer. They're one-piece aluminum with a glossy black paint finish and a stainless-steel lip, and they measure 18x8.5 front, 18x10 rear, with 245/35ZR-18 and 255/40ZR18 BFGoodrich g-Force T/A KDW tires.

Classic Design Concepts' Mustang GT convertible (bottom left) wears Boss Motorsports 338 wheels—20x8.5 front, 20x10 rear—which are available in chrome, black, and gray finishes.

Street Concepts' two-tone 2007 Ford Mustang GT rides on 20x9- and 20x10-inch Maya MR-S wheels with a matte-black face and a gloss-black lip, wrapped in Toyo Proxes T1-R 245/35R20s and 275/30R20s.

Photo courtesy of Street Concepts

Photo courtesy of CDC

Photo © Summit Racing Equipment

Five-Spoke Wheels

The five-spoke remains one of the most popular wheel designs of all time. But have you ever stopped to consider just how many five-spoke designs are on the market today? Here's just a sampling of the possibilities. For instance, the spokes can be straight or twisted, solid or open. Flat, curved, or peaked. Narrow or wide. Polished, matte, painted, or powder-coated.

Photo courtesy of Billet Specialties

Photo courtesy of YearOne, all rights reserved

Photo © Goodguys Rod & Custom Association

Photo by Drew Phillips, courtesy of Granatelli Motorsports

Photo courtesy of Hotchkis

Photo courtesy of Hotchkis

Photo courtesy of Marquez Design

Photo courtesy of Billet Specialties

Photo courtesy of PDK Wheels

Photo courtesy of Performance West Group

Photo courtesy of RideTech

Photo courtesy of Spectre

Chapter 6

Chassis, Suspension & Brakes

1 Time Machines created this one-off Dodge Viper–based independent rear suspension for its '68 *Bullseye* Dart. The center section was constructed from solid billet, and the custom-fabbed setup is loosely based on the Jaguar IRS, with cantilever (horizontally) mounted shocks. *Photo courtesy of Performance West Group*

Street machines and their owners do run the attitude and ambition gamut, from folks who are content chirping (or roasting) the tires and hanging the rear end out around corners to serious handling addicts.

Plus, many of these vehicles are used for everything from grocery-getting to full-on racing, both in a straight line and around corners.

With this in mind, I've gathered an assortment of chassis, suspension, and braking setups that help a wide variety of vehicles accelerate, decelerate, turn, and just plain put the power to the pavement far better than they could in stock form.

2 The Roadster Shop built Barry Blomquist's 1962 Corvette, which rides on the company's new C1 chassis. That chassis and these massive Brembo 6-piston monoblock calipers and 14.5-inch rotors are a big part of the reason this car logged the fastest lap time in the Goodguys/Air Ride Technologies 2009 Street Machine of the Year autocross competition. *Photo © Goodguys Rod & Custom Association*

3 The easy way to convert to an independent front suspension is with a setup like Art Morrison's Weld In IFS Crossmember Kit, which is available in different widths to fit different vehicles. The mandrel-formed 2x4-inch rectangular steel crossmember features fixture-welded steering (for a 1979 to 1993 Mustang rack) and lower control arm attachments. *Photo courtesy of Art Morrison*

4 Mopar's Stage II coil-over suspension kit for new Challengers enables up to a 1.625-inch drop in ride height, as shown here on the 2009 Moparized Challenger. This car also wears 20-inch Mopar Nostalgia Wheels. *Photo courtesy of Chrysler*

5 Hotchkis' 1.5-inch tubular steel lower A-arms for 1970 to 1981 Camaros and Firebirds are more rigid than stock units, with enhanced suspension geometry to dramatically improve handling and control. The TIG-welded, bolt-on pieces have repositioned ball joints for increased caster and an improved camber curve (with -0.6 degrees of camber and +2 degrees of caster built in), providing better stability and traction. *Photo courtesy of Hotchkis*

6 Dave Flynn's new Baldwin-Motion Phase III Camaro started out as a '69 Camaro RS/SS donor. It's now mini-tubbed, and like all Phase III's, it features a Baldwin-Motion Control Freak independent rear suspension, frame connectors, and a tubular front suspension. *Photo by Paul Zazarina, courtesy of Baldwin-Motion*

The Makings of a Mean Mustang

The front K-Member in the *Trans-Cammer* '70 Mustang, built by Grand Touring Garage, is made from 2x4-inch, 0.120-wall mild steel rectangular tubing bent on a five-axis CNC machine by Art Morrison. An oil pan skid plate is mounted to the K-member. The upper and lower A-arms are made from 4130 chromoly tubing with heim ends for caster/camber adjustments. The Mustang also features a Woodward Steering Components front-mounted rack-and-pinion unit, along with the adjustable power servo unit mounted behind the K-member. *Photo courtesy of Grand Touring Garage*

The front suspension includes Penske shocks with remote reservoirs, a hollow front sway bar, and an aluminum sway bar arm with adjustable heim end link. The stepped four-core aluminum radiator is from Ron Davis, and the small triangulated tubing on the front of the chassis is for mounting the fenders and headlamp surrounds. *Photo courtesy of Grand Touring Garage*

The rear undercarriage has flat floor panels. Rear bulkhead air panels and rear-mounted diffuser strakes help with aerodynamics. The center section is a Strange 9-inch with a custom-fabricated housing, Mittler Brothers full-floater axle assembly and ARP wheel studs. The Mustang has a triangular four-bar rear suspension, as opposed to the traditional straight four-bar system used in drag racing. Also shown is the rear driveshaft hoop, which is an integral part of the chassis for both safety and strength purposes. *Photo courtesy of Grand Touring Garage*

All-New Under a Stock-Bodied '57 Bel Air

Dutchman Motorsports' '57 Bel Air rides on the company's new frame, with a Heidt's IFS with polished stainless A-arms, Dutchman independent 12-bolt Chevy rear end, Air Ride Technologies Shockwave air suspension system, Dakota Digital ride height control system, and BFGoodrich tires wrapped around 18- and 20-inch Colorado Custom five-spoke Lazear wheels. For braking, the fabricators went with Wilwood Big Dog six-piston calipers and 13-inch cross-drilled, slotted, and zinc-washed rotors up front, Wilwood four-piston calipers, and 11-inch cross-drilled, slotted, and zinc-washed rotors in the rear. Street & Performance headers and billet motor mount adaptor plates made it possible to install the LS6 Corvette engine, which is topped with a Mech Tech LS supercharger. The beautiful polished stainless mufflers and mandrel-bent tubing are from Magnaflow. *Photos courtesy of Dutchman Motorsports*

7

7 Modern Muscle's '69 and '70 fastback Mustangs come standard with a Heidt's weld-in Mustang II–style front suspension and a Heidt's four-bar rear suspension. An IRS is optional. This car sports Flowmaster mufflers and Afco shocks. *Photo courtesy of Performance West Group*

8 Plum Floored Creations' 2007 Dodge Charger R/T Daytona, called *Plum Floored II*, features a Pedders Track II LX front suspension, including bushings, custom-valved GSR struts and shocks, lowering coils, and sway bars. The rear setup is based on an SRT-8 IRS with an axle cooler. Stopping is via a Baer Brakes Extreme-Plus 6S system. *Photo courtesy of Plum Floored Creations*

9 RideTech's 1970 *SuperNova* sports a Chris Alston's Chassisworks front clip with an Air Ride Technologies Shockwave 16-position adjustable air spring system. The Shockwave mounts like a conventional coil-over replacing both the coil spring and the shock absorber. The *SuperNova*'s rear setup uses Air Rides' AirBar four-link air suspension. An Air Pod compressor system is tucked away in the trunk. *Photo courtesy of RideTech*

10 Mr. Norm's Garage offers bolt-in front suspension kits for A-, B-, and E-body Mopars. The kits come complete with a tubular cradle, tubular control arms, rack-and-pinion power steering, motor mounts, coil-overs, tie rod ends, steering arms, and spindles. This Mr. Norm's '71 Challenger R/T also sports SSBC disc brakes and master cylinder. *Photo courtesy of Performance West Group*

11 Eibach offers its Pro-System-Plus package for a variety of vehicles. Each application is engineered to improve turn-in response, increase cornering speed, and reduce body roll while still retaining excellent ride quality. The kit includes sport springs, bump stops (secondary springs), dampers, and sway bars. There's also a Sport-System-Plus version of the kit with Sportline lowering springs. *Photo courtesy of Eibach*

12 Fatman Fabrications has created a really rigid chassis for 1948 to 1956 F-100s and panel trucks. All mounts for the body, bumpers, radiator, running boards, and bed are provided. The standard suspension and 9-inch rear end with drum brakes is fine for a mild street machine, but Fatman offers a plethora of upgrades, including coil-overs and a narrowed rear end housing. *Photo courtesy of Fatman Fabrications*

13 ProRides and Jimmy Varacalli modified an Art Morrison tube chassis for Summit Racing's '61 Starliner and painted the chassis body color. The rear suspension features an Art Morrison four-link with RideTech Shockwaves, a Speedway Engineering 7/8-inch sway bar, and a Currie 9-inch with 31-spline axles. Braking is accomplished via Wilwood 13-inch rotors with six-piston calipers. *Photo © Summit Racing Equipment*

14 Petty's Garage upgraded the suspension on this 2009 Challenger with Pedders components and then painted the suspension pieces Petty Parts Blue, which is part of BASF's R-M line. Stopping chores are handled by Brembo Gran Turismo brakes. *Photo courtesy of Petty's Garage*

11

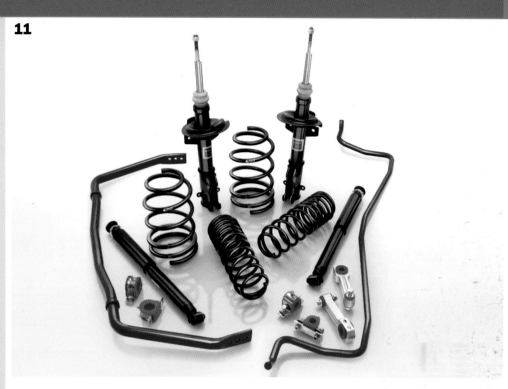

12

13

14

15

15 Hotchkis Performance's subframe connectors for 1968 to 1974 Novas (and other unibody X-cars) are designed to improve handling and traction by reducing chassis flex. You do not have to cut the floorboards to install them. The rear mount must be welded, but the front mount can be bolted or welded. They also come with urethane front body mounts. *Photo courtesy of Hotchkis*

16

16 Art Morrison's Tri 4-Bar Rear Clip Package is intended for street use. It features a triangulated design, with 1 3/8-inch-diameter bars and Morrison poly-bushed stainless-steel rod ends. The package includes a rear sway bar, coil-over shocks, and a 9-inch housing, and the crossmember has passages for the exhaust and for the driveshaft. *Photo courtesy of Art Morrison*

17

18

17 Classic Design Concepts builds the *Bullitt Flashback* '67 Mustang from scratch, sourcing the Phase III coil-over IFS, three-link rear setup, and power rack-and-pinion steering from RRS in Australia. Ride height is adjustable front and rear. Check out the Ford Powertain Applications stainless-steel long-tube headers and CDC-built 2-inch stainless dual exhaust. *Photo courtesy of CDC*

18 Jeffrey's Custom Conversions' Super Street Series stock cars use some NASCAR Car of Tomorrow (COT) technology, particularly in the chassis. The driver can flip a switch on the dash or steering wheel to raise or lower the front or rear in less than 5 seconds. The chassis gets finished in the car buyer's choice of color. *Photo courtesy of Jeffrey's Custom Conversions*

Eaton Differentials

The Eaton Posi limited-slip differential (top row) was offered as a factory performance upgrade for select GM vehicles in the 1960s and 1970s—hence the term Positraction. Eaton still offers the Posi carbon fiber clutch–based differential for a wide variety of street and drag racing applications.

Eaton's Detroit Truetrac (center) was the first aftermarket diff with a fully automatic gear-type limited-slip design (no clutch or friction plates). The helical gears provide quiet and smooth operation while transferring the most torque to the wheel with the best traction. Like the Posi, this universal product provides good traction suitable for drag racing, without affecting handling for everyday street use.

Eaton's Detroit Locker is generally considered a race-only diff, since it maximizes traction by delivering 100 percent of the torque to both drive wheels, though it does have the ability to automatically allow wheel speed differentiation. It's often used by professional drag racers, as well as circle track and off-road racers. It was even voted into the Hot Rod Speed Parts Hall of Fame at the 2008 SEMA Show. *Photos courtesy of Eaton*

19

19 Modern Muscle's '69 Camaro rides on an Art Morrison chassis with C5 Corvette suspension front and rear. That's also a C5 Z06 differential fitted with Rockland Standard 4.10:1 gears. Stopping is handled via SSBC disc brakes, an ABS Powerbrake electric brake booster, and Mocal braided hoses. *Photo courtesy of Performance West Group*

20

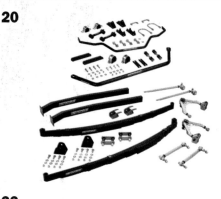

20 Hotchkis offers a variety of Total Vehicle System suspension upgrade kits for muscle cars, including this TVS for 1970 to 1974 Dodge Challengers. The kit includes geometry-corrected upper control arms, adjustable strut rods, adjustable steering rods, front and rear sport sway bars, subframe connectors, and geometry-corrected rear leaf springs. *Photo courtesy of Hotchkis*

21

21 Mr. Norm's '71 Pro Touring 'Cuda rides on an Art Morrison chassis. It features a Strange Engineering Ford 9-inch in the rear, with Afco coil-overs and Stainless Steel Brakes' 13-inch rotors all around (Force 10 calipers in the front, Tri Power three-piston calipers here). *Photo courtesy of Performance West Group*

22

22 Art Morrison's rigid bumper-to-bumper chassis is designed as a replacement for either full-frame or unibody vehicles from 1935 up to the present. Each frame is completely custom made to the buyer's specs with unlimited options to take into account everything from desired ride height to suspension and wheel and tire choices. *Photo courtesy of Art Morrison*

23

23 Roush outfits its 2010 427R Mustang with all-new springs, sway bars, front struts, rear shocks, and jounce bumpers to provide a good balance of comfort and performance. *Photo courtesy of Roush*

Chevelle Update

Pat Hutchins upgraded the front suspension on his '68 Chevelle (top) using Global West's already-assembled G-Plus tubular upper and lower A-arms, which are designed for Pro Touring cars. He also did a simple drum-to-disc conversion using Stainless Steel Brakes' Force 10 SuperTwin lightweight aluminum two-piston calipers and 11-inch slotted and zinc-plated rotors, which will work with 15-inch rims. The kit is available with stock-height or dropped spindles.

In the rear, Global West's double adjustable upper control arms make it possible to adjust the pinion angle. The upper and lower arms also feature a spherical bearing at the front (frame) end to keep the rear end from binding. These frame support braces are beefier than the factory braces to reduce flex. The larger sway bar reduces body roll, and the high-rate coil springs provide better control and lower the back end of the car 3/4 inch.

24

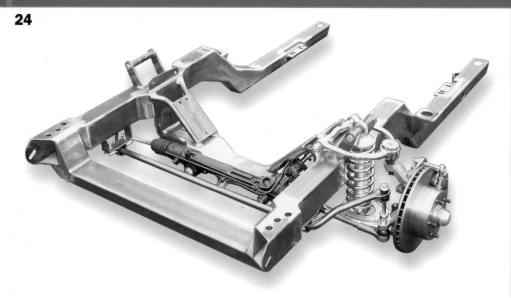

Fatman Fabrications' subframe provides modern suspension for 1967 to 1969 Camaros and Firebirds, and it also fits 1968 to 1974 Novas. You get dramatically better suspension geometry, about 2 more inches of ground clearance, a 2-inch narrower track width, and a lower stance. Fitting a small-block is easy; a big-block requires a little more effort. *Photo courtesy of Fatman Fabrications*

25 Hotchkis has a new Extreme Rear Sway Bar package for first-gen Camaros and Firebirds. Hotchkis created the Chassis Max Rear Sway Bar Brace to tie the subframe together and provide a solid mounting point for the company's rear sway bar. This way, the adjustable 7/8-inch tubular steel sway bar works better and it puts less stress on the factory sheet metal. *Photo courtesy of Hotchkis*

26 RS Performance offers fabricated, fully boxed 1964 to 1972 Chevelle chassis using all stock mounting locations. The Detroit Speed front suspension uses C6 Corvette geometry, including a front sway bar. The large-diameter triangulated four-bar rear suspension adjusts for three ride heights, and comes with a Ford 9-inch housing with 31-spline axles. Engine mounts for small- or big-block Chevys are standard, LS optional. *Photo courtesy of The Roadster Shop*

27 *Plum Floored's '70 Dodge Coronet features a Lateral Dynamics B-body three-link rear suspension with Watts link eliminating leaf springs and using QA1 Carrera coil-overs. A Lateral Dynamics 9-inch housing holds Strange axles and a 3.90:1 limited-slip. The front uses tubular upper control arms, 2.5-inch dropped spindles, MP Super Speedway 1.22-inch torsion bars, a 1.5-inch tubular sway bar, and QA1 Carrera shocks. Photo courtesy of Plum Floored Creations*

25

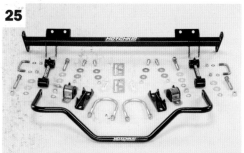

26

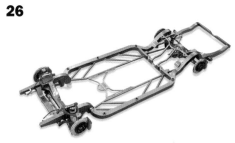

27

Modified Stock Frame

Hulst Customs opted to have Jim Meyer Racing modify the stock frame on this 1956 Bel Air convertible. (Jim Meyer Racing also offers direct-replacement chassis with four-corner stance adjustability.) Hulst then outfitted the frame with custom upper and lower control arms up front and Air Ride Shockwave air springs. The rear setup is not bagged; instead, it features a Kugel billet third member/IRS setup with coil-overs. Check out the way the exhaust is routed through the cross bracing in the frame.
Photos courtesy of Hulst Customs

Chapter 7
Interiors

Lavish luxury. Bare-bones basic. Lightweight for racing. Modern comfort and convenience. Street machine owners clearly have different goals in mind when it comes to the inside of their rides.

In some ways, it's like the muscle car era all over again: Some people want the radio- and heater-delete car, and some want the "gentleman's racer."

Some people want to see a full array of gauges. Some want as little as possible cluttering up a clean dash design.

Some want a stock-looking interior that's subtly updated. Some want every piece clearly and dramatically customized.

That's the beauty of this hobby. You really can have it your way.

2 Hill's Hot Rods built Bob Brandt's '70 Dodge Challenger, with a modern interior by J. D. Glassworks. J. D. cut about 4 inches off the factory seats, then applied charcoal Ultra Leather and gray Ultra Suede with a custom stitch pattern and billet aluminum trim. The metal gauge panel and fiberglass console are custom.

3 Recovery Room Interiors made most of the interior in Mike Guild's '70 Chevelle, with an OEM modern theme. Ron's Restorations built the car. The dash was crafted from aluminum and fiberglass then wrapped in leather with brushed-aluminum trim, and classic Instruments gauges. Recovery Room even wrapped the Lincoln Navigator shift knob and Billet Specialties steering wheel with buckskin Garrett leather. *Photo courtesy of Recovery Room*

4 RideTech's brushed-stainless Tiger Cage roll cage set the theme for the 1970 *SuperNova*'s interior, with matching tubular armrests and trim. The roll cage is a true bolt-in, bolt-together unit. RideTech also replaced the stock instrument panel with Auto Meter GS gauges. The switches on the door are for Nu Relic power windows, and the Cerullo GT Sport Seats feature Crow racing harnesses. *Photo courtesy of RideTech*

5 Lakeside Rods and Rides crafted a fiberglass dash for Flo Hoppe's '62 Impala, which is painted DuPont Hot Hues Lakeside Green to match the body. The Flaming River Waterfall steering wheel is wrapped in leather to match the Dodge Intrepid bucket seats, Corvette shifter, and custom console. Paul Atkins Custom Interiors made the sculpted door panels. *Photo courtesy of Lakeside Rods*

Late-Model Transplant

Modern Muscle's '69 Mustang fastback not only sports a powertrain like that in the new Ford Shelby GT500, it boasts a complete 2006 GT500 dashboard, seats, and console, which the company has swathed in suede and leather. The gauges are from Auto Meter, the carbon fiber steering wheel from Grant. *Photo courtesy of Performance West Group*

6 The interior in the Jim Wangers Signature Edition '69 GTO is built around a pair of Recaro full power, heated and cooled, leather Orthoped seats. The door panels and rear seat were styled to match with body-color top stitching. The Goat features complete Auto Meter Classic Edition instrumentation, A/C, power windows, power door locks, keyless entry, and a sound system with touchscreen navigation. *Photo courtesy of Jim Wangers*

7 The racing stripe on the deck lid flows into the interior of the Baldwin-Motion SuperSpeedster, which started life as a '69 Camaro. The machine-turned panel on the custom console matches the machine-turned instrument panel, and the large hole between the seatbacks channels sound from a pair of 10-inch subwoofers in a sealed box in the trunk. *Photo by Paul Zazarine, courtesy of Baldwin-Motion*

Dash-Top Gauges

Mounting a pod on top of the dash is a clean and easy way to add gauges, and several companies offer components that make this kind of install easy. For instance, Classic Design Concepts' Classic Cluster (top) is a molded gauge pod for 2005 to 2009 Mustangs. It's made from a type of ABS plastic that will not distort in the heat, and it comes in black with a paintable smooth finish. It's a no-drill installation, and it will accept any standard 2 1/16-inch gauges.

For an even more integrated look, Just Dashes can restore a car's original dash pad and fit it with a triple (or larger) gauge pod at the same time. The company will cover the pad/pod either in the original factory-color vinyl with the original grain pattern or in a color to match a swatch you provide. Any standard 2 1/16 gauges will fit. This service currently is available for 1967 to 1969 GM F-bodies, 1970 to 1971 Chevelles and Malibus, 1967 to 1972 Chevy/GMC trucks, 1967 to 1974 Mopar A-bodies and 1968 to 1974 Mopar B-bodies.

8

9

10

11

8 Recovery Room Interiors made these seats specifically to fit Garland Miller, the owner of this Lakeside Rods–built '59 Corvette. The seats are swathed in tan and beechwood Austrian cut calfskin. The dash is reminiscent of the factory design, yet completely custom. The silver trim pieces are aluminum painted with a satin finish. Naiser Racing Components made the steering wheel. *Photo courtesy of Lakeside Rods*

9 Fesler Built outfitted this '67 C-10 pickup with a Tea's Design bench seat, Flaming River steering column, Auto Meter gauges, Electric-Life power windows, and a Kenwood/Kicker sound system. *Photo courtesy of Fesler Built*

10 The '67 *Bullitt Flashback* Mustang from Classic Design Concepts feels vintage, but with all the modern conveniences, including CDC-designed leather-wrapped power bucket seats, tilt steering, and a custom center console with secondary gauges, storage space, cupholders, and air conditioning and power window controls. Under the CDC-designed dash pad, the custom Flashback gauge cluster features Classic Instruments. *Photo courtesy of CDC*

11 Marquez Design outfitted Harold and Sherry Bollenbacher's '69 convertible with their first-gen Camaro interior package, including dash, door panels, and center console. The console is essentially a factory second-gen piece, but Marquez smoothed it and deleted the coin slots on the side, adding a custom shifter opening, hidden ignition, and power window and roof switches. The bucket seats are Recaro Ergomeds. *Photo courtesy of Marquez Design*

Direct Replacements

Classic Instruments offers replacement modern gauge clusters that fit into the stock location for many vehicles, including 1955 to 1956 Chevys (left), 1957 Chevys, 1967 to 1968 Camaros (right), 1969 Camaros, 1967 to 1968 Mustangs, and 1967 to 1972 Chevy trucks. The clusters feature all-electronic instrument movements with a programmable speedo, tach, oil, temperature, voltage, and fuel gauges. *Photos courtesy of Classic Instruments*

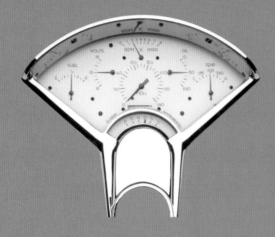

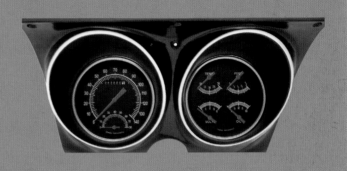

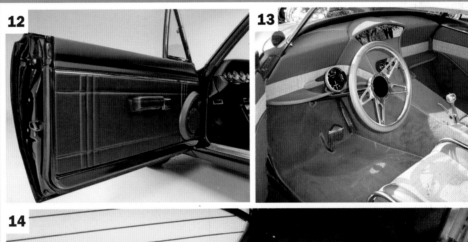

12 For this Pro Touring Dart, Time Machines crafted a more modern, plush interpretation of the original '68 door panels using Ultra Leather. *Photo courtesy of Performance West Group*

13 It's all about priorities: The only gauge that's front and center in Terry Henry's Pro Street '48 Oldsmobile is the tach with shift light. The rest of the instrumentation is relegated to a digital cluster in the center of the dash. Check out those gorgeous pedals and the wicker, leather, and chrome styling theme.

14 Trent's Trick Upholstery crafted the incredibly comfortable-looking interior for Bryan Frank's '69 Pontiac Trans Am, with its unique console. Trent's actually sells those bucket seats, which are covered in leather with contrasting red stitching. The door panels have a transparent red powder-coat finish over stainless trim. *Photo courtesy of Trent's Trick Upholstery*

Tunes in the Trunk

The trunk is the perfect place to stash amps, subwoofers, an extra battery for the sound system, and, of course, actual cargo. Installation styles—and usability—obviously vary wildly. Clockwise from top right: Classic Design Concepts' '67 *Bullitt Flashback* Mustang, Don and Karen Blacksmith's '56 Bel Air built by Hulst Customs, Mouse Prosen's exuberant 2006 Mustang, Bruno's Autoworks' '67 Camaro by Recovery Room (with matching upholstery on the trunk lid), Modern Muscle's '68 Dart.

Photo courtesy of CDC

Photo courtesy of Performance West Group

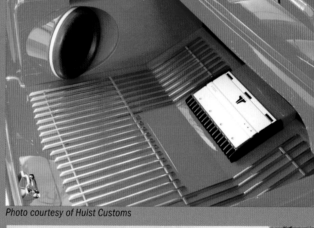

Photo courtesy of Hulst Customs

Photo courtesy of Recovery Room

Photo by Peter Linney, courtesy of ScoCar

15 Gabe's Custom Interiors did a spectacular job of creating a cohesive look for the interior of Don Carlile's '62 Chevy Biscayne, called *Hurricayne.* Check out the beautiful stitch detail work on the front buckets, the rear bench, and the door panels.

16 Modern Muscle's '71 Cuda features a fully custom interior, with Glide Engineering seats, Vintage Air air conditioning and vents, Lokar pedals, a Modern Muscle pistol grip shifter, Sony Xplod entertainment system, and a substantial custom console. *Photo courtesy of Performance West Group*

17 Fesler Built made subtle changes inside this resto-mod '70 Chevelle. Leather replaced the factory vinyl, and it's got Dakota Digital gauges and a Fesler steering wheel. *Photo courtesy of Fesler Built*

18 Marquez Design offers this one-piece headliner for first-gen Camaros and Firebirds, and the company plans to introduce them for a few other vehicles soon. *Photo courtesy of Marquez Design*

19 Trent's Trick Upholstery outfitted its 2010 Camaro with black and textured butterscotch leather—on the seats, the dash, the door panels, the modified factory console, even the custom-heated steering wheel. The custom metal trim is billet aluminum, and the gauge bezels were painted to match.

15

16

17

18

19

High-Tech for High Speed

In place of traditional gauges, RideTech's *Velocity* '68 Camaro sports a fully programmable RacePak IQ3, which contains a 32-channel data logger, 512MB memory card, GPS board, and three-axis g-meter. The center of the Camaro's dash features controls for the Street Challenge air suspension, Vintage Air, and Kicker sound system. Precision Coachworks also installed a seven-speed windshield wiper setup from Detroit Speed. Cerullo upholstered the GT Sport seats in leather with grommets, and Precision Coachworks topped them with custom headrests. *Photos courtesy of RideTech*

Completely Custom

Every part of the interior in the C1RS '62 Corvette is custom. The Roadster Shop hand-formed the seats, the aluminum dash, and the waterfall center console and outfitted the car with a Pioneer navigation system. Classic Instruments made gauges to fit the one-of-a-kind carbon fiber gauge pod. And Recovery Room wrapped the seats in Italian red leather with black Alcantara suede and striking red stitching. The large red button behind the shifter starts the retro/modern car.

Photo © Goodguys Rod & Custom Association

Safety First

Grand Touring Garage built the *Trans-Cammer* '70 Mustang for serious high-speed action, so it features a plethora of safety features, from the big red kill switch on the custom-fabricated aluminum dash to the roll cage (which is covered in leather with Velcro attachments for easy removal) and from the Fire Systems halon fire-suppressor bottle to the 22-gallon Fuel Safe fuel cell. The floorpans and center tunnel were rolled from mild steel and adorned with thermal insulation, while the aluminum custom console is covered in leather. The E-brake handle came from a vintage Jaguar, and the Momo steering wheel has a custom 1940s-style Ford V-8 insignia horn button. *Photos courtesy of Grand Touring Garage*

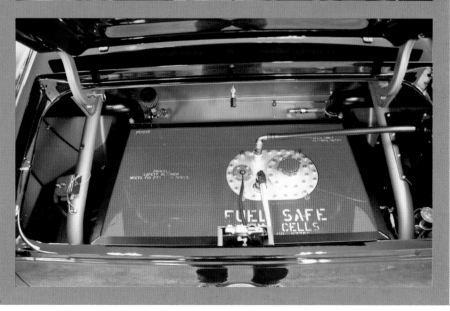

20

20 Recovery Room crafted the interior for Martin McGuire's '57 Chevy, built by Kenny Davis Hot Rods. Tracy Weaver of the Recovery Room starts with 22-inch frames when building custom bucket seats for a Tri-Five. He covered them in Ultra Leather with canvas inserts. With most of the controls on the console, the dash has a clean, almost factory look. *Photo courtesy of Recovery Room*

21 Brett Hunter's '70 Cuda boasts a customized dash out of a Pontiac G6 with a custom console to match and Pontiac Solstice seats. The upholstery's styling was borrowed from a late-model Ferrari, and there's a matching perforated one-piece headliner. *Photo © Goodguys Rod & Custom Association*

22 Several gauge manufacturers offer instruments with custom face designs, like the *Gone in 60 Seconds* speedo made by Classic Instruments for Classic Recreations' *Eleanor* Mustang. *Photo courtesy of Classic Recreations*

A Whole Lotta Console

Lakeside Rods made the full-length center console in Dave and Karen Leisinger's '67 Camaro. Dan Weber covered the Cerullo seats. While the roll cage does make the back seat look somewhat less appealing, the crossbar unpins so it is usable, at least in theory. *Photos courtesy of Lakeside Rods*

Perfect for Tall People

Autoworks International extended the body of Steve Groat's '67 Mustang 7 inches, ditched the rear seat, and positioned the seats far enough back to comfortably accommodate people up to 7 feet tall. Those Recaros are fully adjustable and heated, and they have lumbar support. *The Obsidian SG-One's* dash extends several inches over stock and features Stewart Warner gauges with a Chameleon light package. The touchscreen 10.5-inch LCD monitor provides access to the car's fuel injection system, stereo electronics, and diagnostics, so on a chassis dyno, you can tune the engine from the cockpit. For entertainment, there's a 3,000-watt Kicker system with Dolby 5.1 surround sound, DVD, navigation, MP3, iPod, XM Radio, 60GB hard drive, Bluetooth, and WiFi Internet access. The car also features Formula One–style paddle shifters, Essex luxury carpeting, soundproofing and heat insulation, three-point safety harnesses, and a fire system. *Photos by Nick Nacca, courtesy of ScoCar*

23

24

25

26

23 G. Paul Powell's '54 Corvette features a modernized interior with tan leather on the seats and door panels that wraps around onto the factory dash. The original gauges have been replaced with matching tan-face units from Auto Meter, and the custom waterfall console houses a navigation system.

24 Hulst painted the custom steel floor and topped it with aluminum grates inside this '56 Bel Air. The center console, door panels, and kick panels are fiberglass. That piece between the gauges and the speaker drops down, revealing controls for the Air Ride suspension and Vintage Air. The glove box contains an Alpine head unit. The seats are custom, including steel backs and chrome trim. *Photo courtesy of Hulst Customs*

25 Recovery Room Interiors used fiberglass over aluminum to craft the interior of this '67 Camaro, owned by Bruno's Autoworks. Garrett leather provides the two-tone look, matching the exterior. The lines of the custom, leather-wrapped dash flow into the door panels, featuring grab bars made from oval tubing. The monitor controls the Sony audio/video/nav system. *Photo courtesy of Recovery Room*

26 Top Line Performance built Jim Wilke's '66 Chevelle, and Westminster Upholstery covered the Glide Engineering buckets and stock back seat with black Italian leather. The custom console was painted PPG Lexus Spectra Blue Mica to match the body. *Photo courtesy of Jim Wilke*

27

27 The Glide Engineering seats in Modern Muscle's '69 Camaro are covered in Miami Corporation upholstery, and Miami also provided the carpet. Thermo Tec Interior Insulation helps with temperature, as well as vibration control for the thumpin' Sony audio/video entertainment system. *Photo courtesy of Performance West Group*

Matching Seats

Upholstery Unlimited crafted the interior for The Roadster Shop's '70 Chevelle, including the center console and the trick trim pieces for the floor and doors. The front seats are Cobra carbon fiber units, and the rear seats were custom made to match. They're wrapped in graphite leather with a diamond-stitch pattern that's also carried through to the door panels. The Roadster Shop hand-formed the aluminum dash with its RacePak digital gauge cluster and fabricated a custom roll cage for the car. *Photos courtesy of The Roadster Shop*

28

29

30

28 This Camaro sports impressive custom bodywork, as the deck area on the now-roadster flows smoothly into a full-length center console.

29 Spectre Performance's 1970 mid-engine El Camino was built at So-Cal Speed Shop on Jimmy Shine's TV show *Hard Shine*. Inside, the all-business, go-fast Elky features a clean and simple custom aluminum dash with an array of Auto Meter Pro-Comp Ultra-Lite gauges, plus matching aluminum door panels and lightweight Momo racing seats. *Photo courtesy of Spectre*

30 Here's a truly different option: Dajhan Custom Luxury Interiors will customize a vehicle with precious metals and natural stones, such as lapis, malachite, tiger iron, and petrified wood. *Photo courtesy of Dajhan*

Beyond Racy

The Super Street Series street machines from Jeffrey's Custom Conversions offer a blend of serious NASCAR Sprint Cup equipment and creature comforts. The front bucket seats tilt and slide, and they come with racing-style three-point harnesses. A full complement of Auto Meter Pro Comp gauges lives in the steel dash, and there is a horn button on the quick-release steering wheel. The billet sunvisors are padded, and the head unit for the four-speaker sound system is mounted overhead. Options include leather upholstery, power front buckets, cupholders, and rear seats with three-point harnesses. *Photos courtesy of Jeffrey's Custom Conversions*

A Fascination with Fasteners

Ringbrothers built Erv Woller's '69 Camaro, called *Razor*, including the dash, gauges, pedals, and shifter; then Upholstery Unlimited applied leather pretty much everywhere. The car features Ringbrothers' signature fasteners throughout. And Upholstery Unlimited created nifty storage cubbies for a fire extinguisher and a first aid kit behind the seats/between the roll bars.

Chapter 8
Body & Paint

The caliber of the bodywork and paint in these pages is incredible, and so is the creativity that went into these rides.

You'll find bare metal topped with clearcoat, matte finishes, and glossy paint. Monochromatic done in a modern way. All manner of two-tone paint schemes. Pinstriping. Graphics. Flames.

People put an extraordinary amount of labor into customizing bumpers, windshields, hoods, grilles, and wheel openings. They widened their rides to look tough and fit bigger wheels and tires.

Plus, they made all manner of other functional mods, from adding ducts that aid in brake cooling and hoods that vent heat to front splitters that reduce lift and rear spoilers and diffusers that increase downforce.

2 Grand Touring Garage used a water jet to cut the grille on the '70 *Trans-Cammer* Mustang, finishing it with gray powder coat. To make the grille a focus, they painted the headlight housings and trim gloss black. The air splitter is carbon fiber, as is the one-piece extra-long hood. Windshield tabs reference the Trans-Am era, and the 'glass bumper has been shortened and contoured. *Photo courtesy of Grand Touring Garage*

3 Mr. Norm's 2009 Hemi Cuda convertible was inspired by the super-rare '71 Hemi Cuda ragtop. Convertible Builders transformed the Challenger coupe into a droptop. The car also features Mr. Norm's Cuda-izing components, including the grille and lower grille bars, the shaker hood, the gilled fenders, and the quarter panels. Mr. Norm's completed the look with Hemi billboards. *Photo courtesy of Performance West Group*

4 Wraith Motorsports put about a hundred hours of work into this '68 Mustang's nose alone. The unique front end was designed to be more aerodynamic and provide enough airflow for the 900-horsepower car's blower/intercooler setup. *Photo courtesy of Wraith Motorsports*

Popping the Hood

Modern Muscle created a power-operated, cantilever hood for this '69 Camaro convertible. Push a switch on the console and hydraulic rams lift the hood from the leading edge of the cowl vent slightly first while simultaneously releasing the locking latch. Then the front of the hood lifts. Next, it moves forward over the hood extension and then it lifts up at the back until it completely exposes the engine. The hood can be stopped in any position. The hinges were custom fabricated from billet. *Photos courtesy of Performance West Group*

5 Granatelli Motorsports' twin-turbo 2004 Corvette Z06 features CDC Tiger Shark front and rear fascias, an RKSport carbon fiber hood, and a Catz HID headlight conversion. The flames flowing out of the front brake ducts are a particularly nice touch. *Photo courtesy of ScoCar*

6 Plum Floored Creations tapped Paintshop101 for the body mods on its '70 Dodge Coronet. These include the "power bulge" hood and Coronet R/T–inspired side scoops and side sills that lower and emphasize the body lines. Plus, the front and rear bumpers have been sectioned, chopped, and channeled. SEM's Color Horizons paint is called Plum Floored, just like the car. *Photo courtesy of Plum Floored Creations*

7 Brett Hunter of Hunter Body Shop, Customs & Hot Rods retrofitted his '70 Cuda with a set of modern door handles that work with the car's body lines. *Photo © Goodguys Rod & Custom Association*

Retro, Yet Futuristic

The louvered hood on Ford's Supercharged Thunderbird concept car may be retro, but it's certainly not traditional. The almost futuristic styling features chrome on all of the forward-facing surfaces, and the twin air extractor design does indeed enhance engine cooling. *Photos courtesy of Ford*

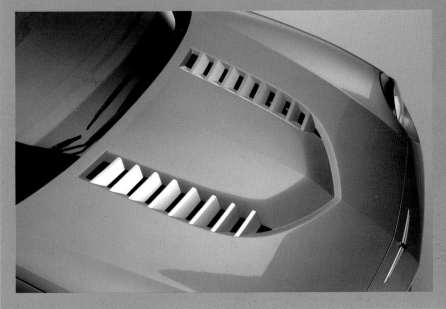

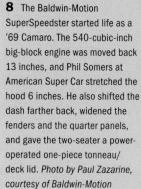

8 The Baldwin-Motion SuperSpeedster started life as a '69 Camaro. The 540-cubic-inch big-block engine was moved back 13 inches, and Phil Somers at American Super Car stretched the hood 6 inches. He also shifted the dash farther back, widened the fenders and the quarter panels, and gave the two-seater a power-operated one-piece tonneau/deck lid. *Photo by Paul Zazarine, courtesy of Baldwin-Motion*

9 Ralph Carungi and Bill Richert wanted a "just pulled out of the back lot" look for their 1954 Lincoln Capri, which had appeared in Robert Mitchum movies. However, since the body was rust-free, they didn't want to go the acid-wash route and rust it. Instead, they had Arizona Color do a complete vehicle wrap using 3M film. *Photo courtesy of Arizona Color*

10 Sometimes I look at a car like this Pro Street Super Rambler and think, "Yeah, why even bother with a hood?" *Photo courtesy of Billet Specialties*

11 CDC's OEM-quality Glassback roof system for 2005-and-newer Mustangs offers a convertible-like view with increased comfort and quiet, plus it provides more headroom than the factory roof. It's formed with two layers of glass like a windshield, and it absorbs solar rays to minimize heat penetration. *Photo courtesy of CDC*

12 Steve's Restorations & Hot Rods spent three days straight painting this '71 Camaro Z28. All of the tribal designs were airbrushed for a three-dimensional effect, and all the colors are PPG Vibrance Custom Color Tri-Coats. Like all top-notch paint jobs, the graphics extend into the door jambs. *Photo courtesy of Steve's Restorations*

Completely Carbon Fiber

World championship drifter Vaughn Gittin Jr.'s 2010 Mustang RTR-C, built by Autosport Dynamics, features amazingly high-quality Epoxy Carbon Composite (ECC) body panels. Every piece—from the grille to the bumpers and from the roof to the door panels—is carbon fiber. Even the HRE CF40 wheels. It's being offered in a very limited edition of 10. *Photos courtesy of Autosport Dynamics*

Re-Envisioning the C1

By the time car owner Barry Blomquist, Phil and Jeremy Gerber of the Roadster Shop, and artist Eric Brockmeyer finished designing the C1RS, it was not so much an updated 1962 Corvette as it was a modern car with vintage styling and some European supercar influence. Every single body component has been heavily massaged or completely replaced.

The team spent hours simply looking at the C1RS, ensuring every body line flowed perfectly. See how the proportions of the hood louvers match the carbon fiber side gills and how the custom lip spoiler out back is a continuation of the rear wheelwell body lines? Not only has the windshield been shortened and leaned back, the lines of its hand-formed aluminum frame flow smoothly into the door trim and the stunning arches behind the headrests.

The tail of the car also is much squarer than original, the quarter panels have been flared, the side coves were removed from the doors, and the entire front end was made fresh from sheet aluminum, including the hood, bumper, grille, and grille surrounds.

Photo © Goodguys Rod & Custom Association

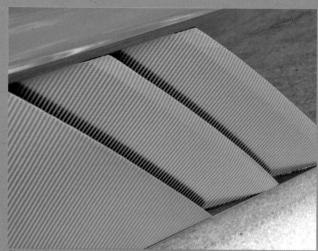

Photo © Goodguys Rod & Custom Association

Photo © Goodguys Rod & Custom Association

Photo © Goodguys Rod & Custom Association

13 Agent 47 is offering the 1969 Harbinger Mustang as a race-prepped roller that definitely could work as a serious street machine. The hood features dramatic air extractors to reduce both drag and lift caused by air flowing through the radiator, which otherwise would get trapped underhood at high speeds.

14 Kirk Johnson liked the proportions on his '68 F-100, but Roseville Rod & Custom still did tons of cleanup, filling seams, shaving trim, cutting down a rear bumper from an Econoline van, pinching the front fenders, changing the angle of the back of the cab, reskinning the doors, and more. It wears PPG Silvertone Silver Metallic paint and GT F-100 stripes reminiscent of a Mach 1 Mustang. *Photo © Goodguys Rod & Custom Association*

15 Lakeside Rods and Rides used a Dynacorn body for Dave and Karen Leisinger's '67 Camaro. The shop removed the stainless window trim and vent windows, installing flush-fit, tinted glass. They also Frenched the bumpers and installed a Corvette Stinger-style fiberglass hood and a hood-mounted tach. The paint is PPG Dover White, silver on the bumpers. *Photo courtesy of Lakeside Rods*

Go Wide

A wide body kit can not only make a car look more aggressive, but it can make room for some serious wheels and tires. For instance, Classic Design Concepts' Group 2 Wide Body package for the 2008-and-up Challenger SRT8 adds 6 inches to the width of the car, making it possible to fit CDC's wheel and tire package: USW three-piece forged wheels (20x10 front, 20x11.5 rear) with Z-rated Pirelli P-Zero Rosso 275/40 and 315/35 tires. The Group 2 Wide Body package includes production-molded composite fenders and rear quarter panel extensions with billboards, inner wheelhouse extensions, and front spoiler canards. The re-arched wheelwells also make the vehicle look lower. CDC outfitted this Challenger with its Heritage Package, which includes a Heritage hood and a shaker cold air system that routes air through the factory airbox and includes a high-flow cone air filter.

Galpin Auto Sports went very wide on this 2010 Mustang convertible, crafting a one-off body kit and then emphasizing the car's new shape with the Pearl Grabber Blue and gloss black PPG paint.

Bomex created the aggressive-looking 2010 Silver Arrow Camaro, which you can buy as a turnkey vehicle or you can get the wide body kit separately. The kit includes widened front and rear fascia, widened fenders, widened quarter panels, widened side skirts, extended door panels, and a rear diffuser.

Photo courtesy of CDC

16 Spectre made the vents on this '70 Mach 1 Mustang functional, so they feed cold air into the fenderwells and then through a Spectre Performance Sidewinder cold air intake system to a bored/stroked 351W (now 408 cubic inches). This setup can drop inlet air temperature significantly. *Photo courtesy of Spectre*

17 Air Ride Technologies' graphic designer, Scott Payton, helped come up with the styling theme for the 1970 *SuperNova*, built by sister company Precision Coachworks. The Nova wears DuPont Hot Hues Butter Nut Yellow paint with clean and simple flat-black graphics, flush-mount glass, and polished-metal trim. *Photo courtesy of RideTech*

18 Aero Collision applied Sherwin-Williams' Planet Color custom paint to Howard Brook's home-built '71 GTX. The color of this paint is much like Plymouth's B5 blue, but it looks radically different because of the new technology and materials in Sherwin-Williams's "optically enhanced" coating. Hence the name: B5 Super Blue. *Photo courtesy of Performance West Group*

19 The Z06 is already lighter than a standard Corvette, and Katech gets the weight down to 2,825 pounds, fully optimized, with its ClubSport package. The carbon fiber front splitter improves aerodynamics, and the matching carbon fiber rear spoiler improves downforce. Plus, the lift-off carbon fiber World Challenge hood vents the engine compartment, reduces weight by 50 percent, and provides more downforce. *Photo courtesy of Katech Performance*

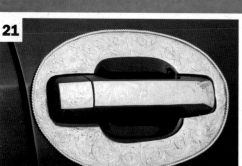

20 A few relatively simple mods—such as removing the trim from the rockers, wheelwells, and side gills; removing the side marker lights and badges; and shaving the door handles and locks—can really modernize the look of a '69 Camaro. *Photo courtesy of Marquez Design*

21 Okay, it may not be a street machine, but the belt buckle–style hand-tooled door handles on Toyota's *Midnight Rider Tundra Tailgater* by Brooks & Dunn are plenty inspiring. *Photo courtesy of Toyota*

22 A matte black racing stripe on a shiny black paint job looks particularly tough on Roush's *Nitemare* F-150. It also draws attention to the Roush hood scoop, with its carbon fiber insert. *Photo courtesy of Roush*

23 Lakeside Rods and Rides performed extensive surgery on Kevin and Karen Alstott's '68 Camaro. They removed the front bumper, rocker panels, door handles, mirrors, side marker lights, and brightwork. They swapped in Harley-Davidson headlights and Marquez Design turn signal indicators, and installed functional brake ducts and a billet grille insert. But the most noticeable change is the carbon fiber hood with a copper scoop. *Photo courtesy of Lakeside Rods*

Big, Bulging Hoods

Some people are all about keeping everything tucked discreetly under a stock-appearing hood. Some folks, not so much. Consider the prominent—and markedly different—hoods on (clockwise from top right) Danny Tyner's '63 Ford Falcon, Plum Floored Creations' '69 Road Runner called *Dark Runner*, Bully Dog's 2010 Camaro, Plum Floored's 1970 Coronet Super Bee called *Mutant Bee*, and Modern Muscle's *Bullseye* '68 Dart.

Photo courtesy of DynoMax

Photo courtesy of Performance West Group

Photo courtesy of Plum Floored Creations

Photo courtesy of Plum Floored Creations

24

25

26

27

24 Classic Design Concepts' hand-built series of Flashback '67 Mustangs start with a Dynacorn body shell. CDC fits them with a one-piece front fascia with brake ducts and driving lights, a heat-extractor hood with integrated turn signals, dual outside sport mirrors (power adjustable, even), and scalloped upper sail panels and lower body side scoops. *Photo courtesy of CDC*

25 Nobody thought a brown car could be cool until Chip Foose unveiled the *Terracuda*. The car's owner, Darren Metropolis, brought in a Breitling watch with a brown face and asked Chip to match the color. He came up with Terracuda Brown, and then custom blended a color called California Gold for the stripes. Both hues are now available from BASF. *Photo by Ryan Hagel, courtesy of Pirelli*

26 DP Classics has a hundred hours of work in the bumpers alone on the company's '71 Chevelle. They're painted a PPG gloss black to match the Steve Van Demon graphics. PPG also custom mixed the three-stage yellow/pearl metallic paint.

27 Street Scene Equipment's 2010 Mustang sports the full complement of components offered by the company, including the GT front urethane fascia, side skirt package, rear valance, three-piece wing, side scoops, window louvers, window ducts, and billet grilles. *Photo courtesy of Street Scene Equipment*

Fiberglass & Metal Combo

Scott Taylor's '68 *Naja* Mustang, which started out as a 1968 A-code fastback, features a labor-intensive combination of sheetmetal panels and a highly reworked *Eleanor* fiberglass body kit—likely one of the last ones Unique Performance pulled together from remaining pieces before the company shut down. Henry's Hot Rods spent countless hours trimming, fitting, and reworking all the fiberglass pieces and then getting rid of any seams, sanding and filling before applying several coats of primer. The car retains the original metal fenders.

The *Eleanor* hood also tapered back to the height of the cowl, so it wouldn't clear the dual Demon carburetors on Scott's engine. Ron Pepper of A Pepper Fabrication restructured the scoop with a 2-inch cowl opening at the rear that also allows for heat dissipation, plus the 'glass hood was strengthened with a metal frame and lengthened 2 inches. Pepper also fabricated the side-opening hood hinges and release pins, hiding the hardware beneath the passenger side inner fender. *Photos courtesy of Scott Taylor*

Velocity Camaro

RideTech's 1968 *Velocity* Camaro features plenty of handcrafted components created by sister company/car builder Precision Coachworks, some of which may eventually make it into production. Most attention-getting are the front splitter, which resembles a NASCAR lower valance, the screens in both valances, and the air diffuser out back. The bumpers have been tucked in snug against the body. They were metal finished and then clear-coated, just like the SS stripes. In fact, the body was so straight on this California six-cylinder car that they could have simply clear-coated the whole thing. Instead, DuPont Hot Hues mixed up a special color, now known as Velocity Orange. Also note the frameless backlight; it's hard-coated Lexan, as is the windshield. *Photos courtesy of RideTech*

28 The body on the *Obsidian SG-One* '67 Mustang was stretched more than 7 inches and slathered in Sikkens Obsidian black paint. Two top-mounted fender intakes provide front disc brake cooling, while flared 1/4-inch panel intakes cool the rear discs. Also note the induction/extraction hood, front valance with twin air intakes, modern headlights and turn signals, and custom side skirts. *Photo by Nick Nacca, courtesy of ScoCar*

29 Steve's Restorations and Hot Rods clearly went crazy on the company's environmentally friendly 1956 F-100. One of the coolest parts, besides the copper grille, is the eco-friendly paint: water-base Vibrance Envirobase from PPG. *Photo courtesy of Steve's Restorations*

30 Ringbrothers swapped in carbon fiber pieces where the side gills used to be on the *Razor* '69 Camaro. The shop also sharpened and elongated the body lines, stretched the wheel openings, and integrated the rear spoiler. Plus, the deck lid and hood are carbon fiber pieces. *Photo © Goodguys Rod & Custom Association*

31 Roush's louvers for the rear quarter windows on 2010-and-newer Mustangs have a classic feel, but a modern look. They're made from high-strength TPO (thermal plastic olefin) using the same high-pressure injection process used by the automakers. They come in factory-matched paint colors or unpainted. *Photo courtesy of Roush*

Wagons

Speaking of bodies, if you want space and you want to be different, you might at least consider building a wagon as your next street machine. Heck, you could go really crazy (and low-buck) and build a four-door.

Photo courtesy of Billet Specialties

Grilles

Photo courtesy of RenovatioLucis.com

Flames

Photo courtesy of Performance West Group

Photo courtesy of Royal Purple

Emblems

Photo courtesy of General Motors

Photo courtesy of Marquez Design

Photo courtesy of Performance West Group

Photo courtesy of Performance West Group

Photo courtesy of Plum Floored Creations

Photo courtesy of RideTech

Photo courtesy of RideTech

Graphics

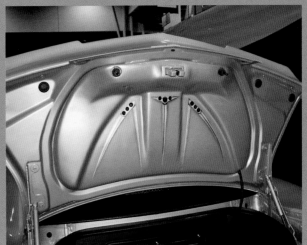

Two-Tone Treatments

Photo courtesy of Billet Specialties

Photo courtesy of Billet Specialties

Photo courtesy of Gearhead Garage

Photo by Rick Head, courtesy of SimiStudio.com

Photo by Ryan Hagel, courtesy of WD-40

Photo courtesy of Trent's Trick Upholstery

Chapter 9
Lighting

People have been mixing and matching headlights and taillights on vehicles since the dawn of the hot rod movement, and street machines are no exception.

In this chapter, you'll find new cars outfitted with vintage lighting and old cars updated with modern equipment. You'll find one-off custom equipment and cleverly repurposed existing pieces.

You'll also find some newer technology, such as LEDs and even new cold cathode fluorescent lighting. These options surely will grow in popularity with car builders as they become more available and more affordable.

2 Marquez Design outfitted the Bollenbachers' '69 Camaro with the company's hand-laid fiberglass lower valance. It's designed to work with Marquez Design's indicators (shown), which are machined from 6061-T6 billet aluminum and which come with amber LEDs. These lights also will work in a stock valance like the factory units, except you'll have to cut new holes. *Photo courtesy of Marquez Design*

3 These Hella taillamps use LED brake lights and turn signals and Hella's own CELIS (Central Lighting Systems) technology for the taillights and parking lights. The easy-install kit is available for late-model Chevy Silverado, Dodge Ram, Ford F-150, and Toyota Tundra trucks, and it includes two LED/CELIS taillamps and a cab-mounted LED brake lamp. *Photo courtesy of Hella*

4 In transforming a 2009 Challenger into a new Hemi Cuda convertible, Mr. Norm's Garage really captured the look of the vintage muscle cars. The car even sports actual 1971 Hemi Cuda taillight assemblies. *Photo courtesy of Performance West Group*

Lighting the SuperNova

The craftsmen at Precision Coachworks not only shaved and narrowed the bumpers on RideTech's '70 Nova, but they also installed a pair of recessed foglights up front, since this car was built for driving, preferably fast. They opted for Marquez Design billet taillights, machine-finished to match the bumper and custom deck lid spoiler. *Photos courtesy of RideTech*

5

5 Classic Design Concepts' hand-built *Bullitt*-style '67 Flashback Mustang features LED taillamps with integrated LED backup lamps. They're mounted in a one-piece rear fascia with an integrated license plate mounting location and flared exhaust shrouds. *Photo courtesy of CDC*

6 The Roadster Shop crafted one-of-a-kind headlight assemblies for this '62 Corvette, with billet trim rings and trick inset turn signals. Plus, the shop used Porsche 997 running lights in the custom grille bar, just below. *Photo © Goodguys Rod & Custom Association*

6

7

7 This 2006 Dodge Charger SRT8 has the Oracle Halo headlight kit from Advanced Automotive Concepts. The "demon eye" kit uses cold cathode fluorescent lighting (CCFL) technology, so the halo rings are rated at 50,000 hours of continuous use. The Sublime Green halos are a nice match to the green pinstripes on the body and wheels and the green wheel calipers.

8

8 Ringbrothers built this '64 Ford Fairlane called *Afterburner* for Kenneth Smith of S&S Cycle. The 20-month build includes an incredible amount of custom work, like these taillights that were machined from 6061 aluminum. So was the gas cap, and the Flowmaster exhaust exits through matching outlets in the custom carbon fiber bumper. *Photo courtesy of Mothers*

LED Lighting Film

LightForm, a new LED lighting "film," makes it easy to bend lighting around corners, over contoured areas, into complicated shapes, and into really tight spaces. Each strip is 10 inches long, 0.5 inch wide and less than 1mm thick. The strips come with red, yellow, blue, or green lights, and they're just as bright at one end as the other. They're a peel-and-stick installation. Besides the strips, the manufacturer plans to introduce a sheet product (shown at right). *Photos courtesy of LightForm*

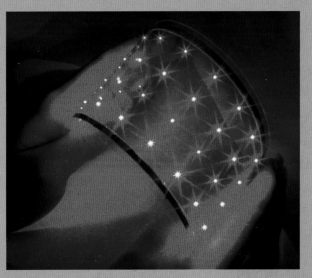

9 Spectre Performance went the Ford Thunderbolt route for the company's 1970 El Camino, removing the inboard headlights from the twin-headlight setup and using those openings to funnel air into the engine. Spectre sells the funnel kit, as well as the SpeedBySpectre 4-inch ProFab QuiKit that makes it possible to design virtually any air intake and intercooler system to work with the funnels. *Photo courtesy of Spectre*

10 Hulst Customs created one-off halogen headlights and running lights with custom buckets and lenses for Don and Karen Blacksmith's '56 Bel Air convertible. The shop also crafted cleaner, more modern-looking taillights, while retaining the stock fuel filler location behind the driver's side lamp. *Photos courtesy of Hulst Customs*

11 Kindig-it Design flush-mounted the taillights in Devan Glissmeyer's '68 Mustang for a much cleaner, more modern look above the sectioned, narrowed, and tucked in bumper.

12 The more shiny stuff you have under the hood, the better neon will look at night. *Photo courtesy of StreetGlow*

13 Marquez Designs outfitted the Bollenbachers' '69 Camaro with the company's 3-D Modern Taillights. The Modern lights have angled vertical bars between the lenses, and those bars have a slight curve to match the profile of the car, unlike the straight bars on Marquez's traditional taillights. The aluminum housing can be finished any number of ways. *Photo courtesy of Marquez Design*

14 While '67 Shelbys came with four 5.5-inch headlights, Scott Taylor's Mustang has the 7-inch headlights used on regular '67 Mustangs, since he prefers the two-headlight/two-foglight look. The foglights, the running lights (inboard of the headlights), and the turn signal indicators are all PIAA units, and the running lights have been Frenched into the fascia.

15 The Roadster Shop fitted BMW Halo headlights to the company's '70 Chevelle. They look way cool, but the installation wasn't easy—it took quite a bit of modification to both the lights and the car.

16 Fesler Built's taillights and backup lights for the '69 Camaro RS fit in the stock locations, but they're made from 6061 billet aluminum. The reverse lights also include LEDs. They're available in several finishes, including natural (shown), brushed, polished, and clear or black anodized. *Photo courtesy of Fesler Built*

17 Grand Touring Garage installed Cibie halogen headlamps in the *Trans-Cammer* '70 Mustang, along with custom-made LED turn signal lamps that mount from the rear for a flush fit. The screened area outboard of the headlamp is blocked off on the passenger side, but it's open here for cockpit fresh air intake. *Photo courtesy of Grand Touring Garage*

18 Lakeside Rods fitted Kevin and Karen Alstott's 1968 Camaro with 1970 to 1973 Camaro taillights from Marquez Design. They come in pairs, and they're machined from solid 6061-T6 billet aluminum and then hand polished. Lakeside Rods added the copper detailing inside the bezels to coordinate with the car's copper and black styling theme throughout. *Photo courtesy of Lakeside Rods*

19 Sound Choice Audio and Performance grafted a set of 1969 Camaro taillights onto the company's 2010 Heritage Camaro. The car also features an all-metal wide body kit that widens it 2 inches in the front, 3 inches in the rear. *Photo by Derek Schimanke, courtesy of SCAP*

20 Four 12-inch neon tubes light up either side of the amps in the trunk of Boston Acoustics' Chrysler 300. Those are two-channel GT amplifiers and 12-inch G Series subwoofers set behind the cool custom grilles. *Photo courtesy of Boston Acoustics*

21 Precision Coachworks built LED taillights for RideTech's *Velocity '68* Camaro. The triple-light design is more like a '69 Camaro than a '68, but clearly this light has been 100 percent reimagined anyway. The outboard lights operate as taillights here. The center lamp in each unit is the brake light. And the inboard lamp is the backup light. *Photo courtesy of RideTech*

Hidden Headlights

The original Plymouth Superbird and Dodge Daytona muscle cars had hidden headlights, and so does Heide Performance Products' Daytona Challenger, based on the 2008-and-up Challenger. But while the vintage cars had vacuum-operated pop-up headlights that were often problematic, this car has doors that drop down to reveal the headlights for better reliability and better aerodynamics. HPP retained the factory Challenger HID lights; the shop just repositioned them to work in this radically different design. *Photos courtesy of HPP*

Chapter 10
Before & After

Ah, the contrast. Nothing illustrates how much time, money, and manpower goes into building a street machine better than a little before-and-after comparo. It's also a great way to appreciate how far we've come in terms of chassis and suspension design, seating and interior materials, engine power output, exterior finishes, wheel and tire design, and so much more.

1 On the left, a stock 1955 to 1957 Chevy chassis. On the right, an Art Morrison Enterprises GT sport chassis. This CAD-engineered-design is surprisingly easy to install; little or no welding is required. It's the same setup found under Art Morrison's GT55, the Bill Mitchell Hardcore 427-powered '55 that *Super Chevy* magazine piloted to 0.94g on the skid pad. *Photo courtesy of Art Morrison*

One of Everything

After spending almost 20 years as a BMW dealership technician, Steve Keefer built his '70 Mustang to help promote his own business, East Bay Muscle Cars. The car needed a lot of work—Steve has more than 2,000 hours of labor into it. He replaced pretty much everything, including the windows, lighting, wiring, brakes, floorpans, shock towers, quarter panels, and rocker panels.

The original 302 got tossed in favor of a highly modified, solid roller-cam 302 with 351 heads. It makes 500 horsepower without nitrous, and Steve added a Nitrous Oxide Systems 150-shot Sportsman Fogger just in case. He also swapped the original C4 automatic for a Top Loader four-speed, and he created a custom fuel system.

Steve ditched the original leaf spring setup out back in favor of a Total Control four-link suspension, plus he extended the rockers 1 1/4 inches to hide the suspension mounting points.

Inside, Steve replaced all the factory wood grain with aluminum-finished trim for a more modern look, and he installed an updated gauge cluster with Auto Meter instrumentation. The tired factory buckets were replaced with Corbeau seats covered in microsuede.

Outside, the paint is Toyota Red Salsa Pearl with Lexus silver, and the gray-powder-coat trim is finished with satin clear. The matching wheels are 18x9 and 19x10 Budnik Cannons with 255/40-18 and 295/35-19 BFGoodrich KDWs.
Photos courtesy of East Bay Muscle Cars

Old School to New School

This '63 Corvette convertible arrived at HiTek Hot Rods with a vintage 327/340-horsepower small-block under the hood, and it left with a 430-horsepower modern EFI LS3 small-block. Ordinarily, this swap isn't as easy as changing from one vintage Chevy engine to another; however, HiTek also slid a Street Shop Inc. chassis under the 'Vette, and the chassis had been set up to accommodate an LS engine. To make it work, HiTek used a GM LS3 controller kit, along with headers and motor mounts from Street & Performance.

The accessory brackets and pulley system can pose a problem for this kind of installation, so HiTek wound up mixing and matching Street & Performance brackets and pulleys, then the shop heavily modified an A/C compressor and bracket and a water pump. Vintage Air's Front Runner setup wasn't available at the time, but it simplifies this swap. *Photos courtesy of HiTek Hot Rods*

Bolt-On Handling Kit

Want to know how much of a difference a bolt-on handling kit can make? Check out the before and after shots of Joe Molina's 1966 Chevy Caprice 396 wagon.

Joe had given the car a makeover in the early 1990s, which included chopping the springs to lower the ride height, adding some basic performance bolt-ons to the big-block, and swapping the steel wheels for 17-inch Enkei five-spokes. Not exactly the recipe for a g-machine.

To update *Popz Wagon*, Molina had Hotchkis Sport Suspension install its B-Body Chevy Total Vehicle System (TVS) suspension kit, with an adjustable tubular steel heavy-duty sway bar and optional sport coil springs and Hotchkis HPS1000 shocks. Molina also ordered a Hotchkis steering rebuild kit, which includes new heat-treated forged ball joints, tie rod ends, center links, idler arm, and pitman arm.

Out back, the car was fitted with heavy-duty Hotchkis high-performance upper and lower control arms, which radically reduce body motion and improve traction and handling, as well as a large rear sway bar that cuts body roll. The adjustable panhard bar helps dial-in the rear end on lowered vehicles, and new springs evened out the ride height, which had sagged and become nose-high on the old worn-out coils.

The difference in handling is dramatic. It's still not totally flat through the corners, but it's a whole lot more fun to drive on the street. *Photos courtesy of Hotchkis*

Cuda Revival

When Shawn Williams of Street Concepts found this '71 Cuda, it was really rough. Every panel on the car had to be repaired or replaced, which he did during a rotisserie rebuild using YearOne resto pieces. He also added flush-mount taillights and a shaker hood scoop. Fix Auto Collision prepped and painted the car House of Kolor Lava Red, and Cal Bumpers refinished the bumpers.

Shawn also ditched the tired 318 engine, 727 trans, and 8 3/4 rear end in lieu of a Mopar fully polished 540-cubic-inch aluminum crate Hemi with an NX Direct port nitrous system good for 700 horsepower, a Bowler-built 727 with Gear Vendors under/overdrive, and a Speedway Engineering SuperMax quick-change rear end. To handle the extra power, he upgraded the suspension with a Magnumforce front tubular setup and a custom-fabricated Street Wize four-link rear, and also installed custom subframe connectors and Wilwood brakes.

The Cuda now rides on 20x8.5 and 20x11.5 GFG Kliessig 5 wheels with 255/30R20 and 295/30R20 Toyo T1-R tires. The interior features Cobra Sidewinder seats and a custom aluminum console wrapped in leather by Bill Dunn's Auto Upholstery, along with Stewart Warner gauges, A/C by Classic Auto Air, and a Kenwood head unit with MB Quartz speakers, subs, and amps. *Photos courtesy of Street Concepts*

Nostalgic versus Modern

Nothing like placing a shot of a street machine next to a vintage factory photo for a little compare and contrast.

How many modifications can you spot on Garland Miller's '59 Corvette, built by Lakeside Rods and Rides?

Photo courtesy of General Motors

Photo courtesy of Lakeside Rods

Resources

Aero Collision & Fabrication
Lancaster, NY
716-685-AERO

Agent 47
Carlsbad, CA
760-496-3809
www.agentfortyseven.com

American Super Car
Hudson, FL
727-863-6800
www.americansupercarinc.net

A-One Auto Body Shop
Huntington Beach, CA
714-848-3001

A Pepper Fabrication
Sacramento, CA
916-802-0785
www.pepperfab.com

Arizona Color
Phoenix, AZ
623-580-7386
www.arizonacolor.com

Arrington Engines
Martinsville, VA
866-844-1245
www.shophemi.com

Art Morrison Enterprises
Fife, WA
866-321-4499
www.artmorrison.com

Autosport Dynamics
Charlotte, NC
704-509-4660
www.autosportdynamics.com

Baldwin-Motion
Bradenton, FL
941-713-8443
www.officialbaldwinmotion.com

Banks Power
Azusa, CA
800-601-8072
www.bankspower.com

Barris Kustom Industries
North Hollywood, CA
818-984-1314
www.barris.com

Barry's Speed Shop/SRRC
Corona, CA
951-273-9284
www.barrywhitesrrc.com

Basko Engine Service
Gilbert, AZ
480-967-1956

Bill Dunn One Stop Shop
Huntington Beach, CA
714-848-3985
www.bill-dunn.com

Billet Specialties
La Grange, IL
800-245-5382
www.billetspecialties.com

Bill Mitchell Hardcore Racing Products
Ronkonkoma, NY
631-737-0372
www.theengineshop.com

Bomex
Gardena, CA
310-527-3111
bomexaeroco.com

Boss Motorsports
www.bossmotorsports.com

Boston Acoustics
201-762-2100
www.bostonacoustics.com

Bowler Performance Transmissions
Lawrenceville, IL
618-943-4856
bowlertransmissions.com

Bruno's Autoworks
Omaha, NE
402-597-9820
www.brunosautoworks.com

Butler Performance
Leoma, TN
866-762-7527
butlerperformance.com

Bryant Racing
Anaheim, CA
714-535-2695
www.bryantracing.com

Bryce Customs
www.b2cars.com

BS Industries
North Hollywood, CA
877-527-9327
bodiestroud.com

California Pony Cars
Ontario, CA
888-225-7669
www.calponycars.com

Callaway Cars
Old Lyme, CT
860-434 9002
www.callawaycars.com

Cedardale Auto Upholstery
Mount Vernon, WA
360-424-7961

Cherry Bomb
Loudon, TN
866-869-9704
www.cherrybomb.com

Chicane Sport Tuning
Torrance, CA
310-782-0063
www.chicanesport.com

Chris Alston's Chassisworks
Sacramento, CA
888-388-0297
www.cachassisworks.com

Classic Automotive Restoration Specialists
(CARS Inc.)
Rochester, MI
800-CARS-Inc
www.carsinc.com

Classic Design Concepts (CDC)
Novi, MI
866-624-7997
www.classicdesignconcepts.com

Classic Instruments
Boyne City, MI
800-575-0461
www.classicinstruments.com

Classic Recreations
Yukon, OK
877-235-3266
www.classic-recreations.com

Mike Cooper
www.michaelcooper.us

Curtis Speed Equipment
Fallbrook, CA
888-471-8473
www.curtisspeed.com

D&P Classic Chevy
Huntington Beach, CA
800-647-1957
www.dpchevy.com

Dajhan Custom Luxury Interiors
Montebello, CA
323-717-8918
www.dajhan.com

Detroit Speed & Engineering
Mooresville, NC
704-662-3272
www.detroitspeed.com

Dutchman Motorsports
Portland, OR
503-257-6604
www.dutchmanaxles.com

East Bay Muscle Cars
Brentwood, CA
925-516-CARS
www.eastbaymusclecars.com

Fatman Fabrications
Charlotte, NC
704-545-0369
www.fatmanfab.com

Fesler Built
Scottsdale, AZ
480-748-2000
www.feslerbuilt.com

Flowmaster
Santa Rosa, CA
800-544-4761
www.flowmastermufflers.com

Forgiato Designs
Sun Valley, CA
818-771-9779
www.forgiato.com

Gabe's Street Rods Custom Interiors
San Bernardino, CA
909-884-5150
www.gabescustom.com

Galpin Auto Sports
Van Nuys, CA
877 GO-GAS-GO
www.galpinautosports.com

Gearhead Garage
Sacramento, CA
916-481-CARS
www.gearheadgaragecars.com

Goodguys Rod & Custom Association
Pleasanton, CA
925-838-9876
www.good-guys.com

Granatelli Motorsports
Oxnard, CA
805-486-6644
www.granatellimotorsports.com

Grand Touring Garage
North Bend, OR
541-759-2454
www.grandtouringgarage.com

Griffin Interiors
Bend, OR
541-389-8612

Griggs Racing
Petaluma, CA
707-939-2244
www.griggsracing.com

Hedman Hedders
Whittier, CA
562-921-0404
www.hedman.com

Heide Performance Products
Madison Heights, MI
248-307-4263
www.hppcars.com

Henry's Hot Rods
916-852-6350
www.henryshotrod.com

Hensley Performance
Knoxville, TN
865-947-0426
www.hensleyperformance.com

Hillbank Motor Sports
Irvine, CA
888-445-5226
www.hillbankmotorsports.com

Hill's Hot Rods
Lubbock, TX
806-866-0586
www.hillshotrods.com

HiTek Hot Rods
Dayton, OH
937-277-9488
www.hitekhotrods.com

Hot Rods & Custom Stuff
Escondido, CA
760-745-1170
www.hotrodscustomstuff.com

Hulst Customs
Merlin, OR
541-474-1980
www.hulstcustoms.com

Hunter Body Shop, Customs & Hot Rods
Edina, MO
660-397-3346
www.hunterbodyshopmo.com

Jeffrey's Custom Conversions
North Syracuse, NY
315-458-0837
jeffreyscustomconversions.com

JF Kustoms
Osoyoos, British Columbia
250-495-3328
www.desertspeedshop.com

Johnson's Hot Rod Shop
Gadsden, AL
256-492-5989
www.johnsonshotrodshop.com

Jon Kaase Racing Engines
Winder, GA
770-307-0241
www.jonkaaseracingengines.com

Just Dashes
Van Nuys, CA
800-247-3274
www.justdashes.com

Katech
Clinton Township, MI
866-KATECH1
www.katechengines.com

Keith Craft Inc.
Arkadelphia, AR
870-246-7460
www.keithcraft.com

Kenny Davis Hot Rods
Rogers, AR
479-936-4395
www.kdhotrods.com

Kim Barr Racing Engines
Garland, TX
972-272-6121
www.kimbarrracingengines.com

Kindig-It-Design
Salt Lake City, UT
801-262-3098
www.kindigit.com

Lakeside Rods and Rides
Rockwell City, IA
712-297-8671
www.lakesiderodsandrides.com

Lingenfelter Performance Engineering
Decatur, IN
260-724-2552
www.lingenfelter.com

Little Joe's Rod Shop
Denver, NC
704-489-1937
www.littlejoesrodshop.com

Magna Charger
Ventura, CA
805-289-0044
www.magnacharger.com

MagnaFlow Performance Exhaust
Rancho Santa Margarita, CA
800-824-8664
www.magnaflow.com

Marquez Design
West Sacramento, CA
916-373-9783
www.marquezdesign.com

Mast Motorsports
Nacogdoches, TX
936-560-2218
www.mastmotorsports.com

Max Nealon
max@cncpics.com

Michael's Rod Shop
Franklinville, NC
336-498-2715
www.michaelsrodshop.com

Modern Muscle
Hudson, FL
727-869-9533
www.realmodernmuscle.com

Mr. Norm's Garage
Hudson, FL
727-869-9533
www.mrnormsgarage.com

Nelson Racing Engines
Chatsworth, CA
818-998-5593
www.nelsonracingengines.com

Oasis Luxury Alloys
Anaheim, CA
714-533-3286
www.oasiswheels.com

Paul Atkins Interiors
Hanceville, AL
256-352-9608
www.paulatkinsinteriors.com

PDK Wheels
Chicago, IL
800-PDK-2822
www.pdkwheels.com

Performance Associates
San Dimas, CA
909-592-4441
www.pahorsepower.com

Performance West Group
Bonsall, CA
760-630-0547
www.performancewestgroup.com

Picture Car Warehouse
Los Angeles, CA
213-534-3775
www.picturecarwarehouse.net

Plum Floored Creations
Phoenix, AZ
623-986-5000
www.plumfloored.com

Pratt & Miller Corvette C6RS
www.prattmillerc6rs.com

Precision Coachworks
Jasper, IN
812-482-4313
paintgods.com

Precision Turbo & Engine
Hebron, IN
219-996-7832
www.precisionturbo.net

PSE Superchargers
Edmond, OK
877-349-0790
www.pse.us

Pure Vision Design
Simi Valley, CA
805-522-2232
www.purevisiondesign.com

Purpose Built
Sacramento, CA
888-40-BUILT
purposebuilt.com

Rad Rides by Troy
Manteno, IL
815-468-2590
www.radrides.com

Ray Barton Racing Engines
Robesonia, PA
610-693-5700
www.raybarton.com

Razzi
Alpharetta, GA
800-235-6087
razzi.com

Recovery Room Hot Rod Interiors
Plattsmouth, NE
402-235-3800
recoveryroomrodinteriors.com

Reilly MotorSports
White Haven, PA
570-443-7440
www.reillymotorsports.com

Renteria Brothers Custom Shop
Morgan Hill, CA
408-779-2884

Rick Bottom Designs
Mendota, IL
815-539-6487

Ringbrothers
Spring Green, WI
608-588-5377
www.ringbrothers.com

Roadster Shop
Mundelein, IL
847-949-RODS
www.roadstershop.com

Rock's Rod & Custom
816-210-4834
rocksrodandcustom.com

Ron Mangus Interiors
Rialto, CA
909-877-9342
www.ronmangusinteriors.com

Ron's Motorworks
Bernie, MO
573-293-5350
ronsmotorworkscustoms.com

Ron's Restorations
www.ronsrestoration.com

Roseville Rod & Custom
Roseville, CA
916-784-3931
www.rosevillerodandcustom.com

Roy Brizio Street Rods
South San Francisco, CA
650-952-7637
www.roybriziostreetrods.com

RPM Hot Rods
Warrendale, PA
724-940-3322
www.rpmpgh.com

Ryan Hagel
www.rchdesigns.com

Sanderson's Customs and Conversions
888-474-6777
sandersoncc.com

Santini Paint & Body
Westminster, CA
714-891-8895
www.santiniusa.com

ScoCar
Carrollton, TX
972-417-1900
www.scocar.com

Smeding Performance
Rancho Cordova, CA
877-639-7637
www.smedingperformance.com

So-Cal Speed Shop
Pomona, CA
909-469-6171
www.socalspeedshop.com

Sound Choice Audio and Performance
Grand Island, NY
716-775-3333
www.scapusa.com

Spectre Performance
Ontario, CA
909-673-9800
www.spectreperformance.com

SRIII Motorsports
New Lenox, IL
815-462-4138
www.sriiimotorsports.com

Steve's Auto Restorations
Portland, OR
503-665-2222
www.stevesautorestorations.com

Steve's Restorations & Hot Rods
Marcy, NY
315-733-3393
stevesrestorations.com

Strange Motion Rod & Custom
Construction
www. strangemotion.com

Street Concepts
Anaheim, CA
714-630-3030
www.streetconcepts1.com

StreetGlow
Wayne, NJ
800-787-3384
www.streetglow.com

Street Scene Equipment
Costa Mesa, CA
888-477-0707
www.streetsceneeq.com

Strut
San Clemente, CA
949-361-9841
www.strutwear.com

Summit Racing
Tallmadge, OH
800-230-3030
www.summitracing.com

Thom Taylor
www.thomtaylordesigns.com

Time Machines
Hudson, FL
888-869-9577
www.timemachinesinc.com

Tim McAmis Race Cars
Hawk Point, MO
636-338-4912
www.timmcamis.com

Trent's Trick Upholstery
Baltimore, OH
740-468-2727
www.trentstrickupholstery.com

Turn Key Engine Supply
Oceanside, CA
760-941-2741
www.turnkeyenginesupply.com

Upholstery Unlimited
Clinton, IA
563-242-7607
www.wecoveritall.biz

VanGordon Racing
Upland, CA
909-946-5991
www.vangordonracing.com

Lamar Walden Automotive
Doraville, GA
770-449-0315
www.lamarwaldenautomotive.com

Wegner Motorsports
Markesan, WI
920-394-3557
www.wegnerautomotive2.com

Wraith Motorsports
Atlanta, GA
770-605-4760
www.wraithmotorsports.com

YearOne
Braselton, GA
800-Year-One
www.yearone.com

Index